TRANSPIRATIONS

Guidance for the Head & Heart
through Career and Beyond

Thomas Bachhuber, Ed.D.

Published 2021 / The Center for Life Transitions

Printed in the United States of America

(MOBI) E-ISBN: 978-0-578-60435-0

(EPUB) E-ISBN: ISBN-13: 978-0-578-60434-3

PRINT: ISBN-13: 978-0-578-80445-3

Transpirations: Guidance for the Head and Heart through Career and Beyond, 2nd Edition

Written by Thomas Bachhuber

Caritas Communications
Mequon, WI 53092
dgawlik70@gmail.com

DEDICATION

To Les—for her love, wisdom and strength over almost 50 years. She makes anything anyone writes better. She surely did with this work.

And   in gratitude for her, Libby, Emmy, Jay, Christopher, Seth, Chuck, Jennifer, and the brand new Oona Mae Harper Bachhuber. Because family matters most.

TRANSPIRATIONS

IN APPRECIATION

There are so many people to thank. First, to my spouse LESLIE of 50 years, for her love and courage in giving me the freedom to pursue meaningful work. I know it was not always easy for her. And to our kids LIBBY, EMILY, and JAY who have cheered for me no matter what crazy thing I was pursuing.

Thanks to the Board of the Center for Life Transitions for supporting the book as an important part of our Center mission: CHUCK HAYS, JOHN GLASER, CONNIE POPP, SANDY WYSOCKI and TOM LULJAK.

To TERRI for her creativity and professionalism in designing the Center brand, which included the seasonal tree used for the cover.

To KRISTAL for her cleverness and talent in enhancing the seasonal tree for the cover, and for all the wonderful artwork she's done over a decade plus on a wide collection of my projects.

To YESH who encouraged me to write the *TRANSPIRATIONS* Newsletter, the basis for the book. And for the title!

To ROBERT GOTCHER, PH.D. Professor at Sacred Heart Seminary and School of Theology, for his encouragement and guidance early in the process.

To DAVID GAWLIK, Publisher of Caritas Communications, for believing in me and this work from the beginning. And for his understanding and expertise throughout the journey.

For the Reviewers

BILL BANIS—Your support throughout our career paths has been extraordinary. You and Jim Briggs are the only people I know who had the skills, fearlessness and intellect to leap from career director to VP, which we in the field know is a colossal accomplishment.

JACK BENNETT—Where have the years gone, new and old friend from Ripon College? You have charted a life course to be proud of; father, husband, educator, coach and Christian man. And good friend to many, of whom I'm happy to say I'm one.

JIM BRIGGS—Reconnecting our relationship and work has been a highlight for me during this "purposeful age" for each of us. You are a great partner and friend.

KAREN DOWD—We go back a long ways to an early MCPA meeting. Our synergy on the professional, personal and spiritual has been uniquely meaningful. I'm grateful for its continuation.

JIM FLAHERTY—Your spiritual and educational work at Marquette and Gesu has impacted hundreds, thousands! Thank you for your warm welcome whenever I asked for help. Including this newest project.

CHUCK HAYS—VP of the Center Board, seasoned expert in employment and transition coaching. My dear friend and number one guide for all Center initiatives. Thanks Buck.

MONICA MEAGHER—Ignatius and all he stands for came alive through you. I'm immeasurably grateful for your collaboration in work, your mentoring my spirituality and most importantly, your friendship.

GENE MERZ—You introduced me to another Tom Bachhuber, a Jesuit professor who wrote a book on logic! I'm grateful for your presence and guidance. And your book *Moment by Moment* engaged my faith like no other. Your genuine support of this work warms my heart.

PARKER PALMER—Your wisdom for tens of thousands over decades is only surpassed by the personal kindness which emanates toward your devotees. The counsel you've provided me directly, through your work and now, your support for this writing is cherished beyond words.

ROBERT PAVLIK—Your leadership, friendship and guidance through the Quaker clearness exercise encouraged my focused energy to do this book. I'm looking forward to continued breakfasts at Miss Katie's Diner.

JOYCE RUPP—Sister Joyce, what can I say? Your compassion in meeting my Mom and Dad over coffee blessed their lives with deep richness. Your affirmation of my work is very moving.

DENISE DWIGHT SMITH—You know college students like few others so your recognition of this book's value to them is treasured. Our connection surpasses time and industry; our friendship is special.

TRANSPIRATIONS

PRAISE FOR TRANSPIRATIONS

PARKER J. PALMER, PH.D.

"Transitions are a constant in our lives. Time after time, we find that the old maps don't work, and we must reach deep into our spiritual resources to find the guidance we need. TRANSPIRATIONS—transitions inspired by the spirit—is what Tom Bachhuber calls these passages, and he should know. For decades he has been helping people make their transitions in a life-giving way, moving beyond fear to faith on to solid ground. The illustrations in this book, some from Tom's own life, are real and compelling, and the exercises he recommends are immediately helpful. The reader soon learns that he or she is on pilgrimage with a good and grounded man, not on a "magical mystery tour" with a flighty spinner of tall tales. I recommend this book for all who are seeking to take their next turn in life in a way that responds to the imperatives of their souls."

Parker Palmer is the founder and Senior Partner of the *Center for Courage & Renewal,* which oversees the "Courage to Teach" program for K-12 educators across the country and parallel programs for people in other professions, including medicine, law, ministry and philanthropy.

He has published a dozen poems, more than one hundred essays and eight books including *Healing The Heart Of Democracy: The Courage To Create A Politics Worthy Of the Human Spirit, A Hidden Wholeness: The Journey Toward An Undivided Life,* and *Let Your Life Speak: Listening For The Voice Of Vocation.* Palmer's work has been recognized with thirteen honorary doctorates, two Distinguished Achievement Awards from the National Educational Press Association, an Award of Excellence from the Associated Church Press, and grants from the Danforth Foundation, the Lilly Endowment and the Fetzer Institute.

JAMES BRIGGS

"This book is a beautiful and inspiring integration of Tom's personal experiences, reflections and insights from favorite spiritual writers and poets, and the wisdom and guidance needed for navigating life's transitions, especially toward work that provides meaning and purpose. The work is a masterful reflection on the lessons and wisdom that flow from life's joys and sorrows, dreams and challenges—all from a perspective of high hope for new beginnings no matter what they might be or when they might occur over the course of one's life. The connection Tom makes between his personal experiences—serious illness, the loss of his parents, and the birth of his first grandchild and the experiences of job hunters and career changers are both insightful and helpful. A hidden gem lies concealed in the Appendix. *Twenty-two Random Ideas on Making Successful Career/Work Transitions* is worth its weight in gold to anyone in the midst of a career transition."

Jim is the retired Executive Director of the *School of Applied Theology* and former Executive Assistant to the President and Vice President of Student Services at Santa Clara University. Prior to his five years at SAT and his 22years at SCU, Jim was Director of Career Planning and Placement at the University of California Berkeley and Georgetown University. Jim's present ministry includes coaching and workshop leadership on spirituality and purposeful aging.

JOYCE RUPP

"What a superb book Thomas Bachhuber has created. This marvel-ous, balanced book contains a combination of mind and spirit, the wisdom from Tom's personal experiences and the insights of other authors, spirituality for inspiration and practicality for activation. This book flows like a river, carrying encouragement and hands-on application for readers to identify the issues, go deeper, become clearer, set goals, and stay hopeful. I highly recommend this book to anyone experiencing career or retirement transitions."

Sister Joyce Rupp, O.S.M., is an award-winning author who is also a retreat and conference speaker. She is the co-director of *The Institute of Compassionate Presence,* a member of the Servite Order, and a volunteer for Hospice. Her books include *Walk in a Relaxed Manner, Circle of Life* and *Little Pieces of Light* among many others.

ROBERT A. PAVLIK, PH.D.

"Thomas Bachhuber brilliantly develops William Bridges' three stages of transition, Endings, Middles, and Beginnings into the three chapters of TRANSPIRATIONS. Tom's book is an authentic call to be mindful, hopeful and confident of God's presence in making such transitions for our careers and work.

Tom shares several journal entries for significant ending, middle and beginning times in his personal and professional life. Tom then shares his own reflections and presents the voices of many theologians, poets, philosophers, Biblical characters and persons seeking new work in order to inspire and remind us of ways to build our own wisdom, voice and courage for our own work transitions. Whether I read a chapter at a time or open the book to random parts, I am humbled by Tom's honesty and vulnerability in his journal entries, inspired by his Reflections For Work, and both challenged and affirmed by his guidance for pondering and discerning the next things I can do.

TRANSPIRATIONS is helping me to look at myself and others in new loving and courageous ways especially when fear, impatience or quick fixes are involved. I am developing new language, networks and possibilities when I am frustrated and skeptical. I am learning to act from gratitude and other healthier parts of my being when I am taking my next steps in my career."

> Dr. Bob Pavlik serves as the Executive Director of the *High Wind Foundation* which funds partnerships for sustainability, applying his areas of expertise in literacy, learning and community development for the Sustainability Movement. He has taught graduate courses at the University of Northern Colorado and Cardinal Stritch University where he also served as Director of Faculty Development. For the last 15 years, he directed the *School Design and Development Center and the Project for Community Transformation* at Marquette University.

JAMES FLAHERTY, S.J., PH.D.

"Tom Bachhuber has written an excellent resource for people making important transitions in life. He has done so by employing a multi-level approach of the professional, the psychological, the personal(his own life transitions of illness and loss), and finally, the spiritual. It is rare to find a work that incorporates all such levels,especially the spiritual. The latter is most significant in that it provides the wisdom and faith to sustain us in what is often a challenging but ultimately rewarding process."

Dr. James Flaherty, S.J. is Pastor at Gesu Church, the Jesuit parish of Marquette University and former Professor in the Marquette University Philosophy Department. He is a member of the Board of Trustees of Marquette University and Santa Clara University.

CHARLES D. HAYS

"I recommend TRANSPIRATIONS as a unique resource which can be highly effective as a companion to traditional job search books. Tom has utilized the well respected William Bridges model in creating a unique framework connecting the abstract—spirituality— with the pragmatic—job search. His writing offers an intriguing combination of heartfelt personal experiences related in a fashion that projects wisdom, insight and humor together with very useful advice on the career transition process. Tom's distinctive dualistic approach conveys the message to the reader that there are no "quick fixes" to the transition process, but that it is conceptually a part of life's inner journey."

> Charles Hays is a retired Vice President, Right Management Consultants, Inc. the world's premier career transition firm. He has extensive experience in coaching executive, managerial and professional level individuals in the areas of career strategic planning, re-employment and entrepreneurship and retirement planning for over thirty years.

DENISE DWIGHT SMITH

"I heartily endorse this book as a tool for anyone in a career transition. Students in college looking to the future can especially excel from using this engaging read and story based text which prompts very important questions they each need to address. The book is invaluable for those feeling stuck in decision making, and a perfect aid for necessary reflection and getting to the next step. The process by which you use this resource is a skill development forming tool in and of itself. Translating one's academic background, and personal experiences, and skills all lead to the dream career when these insights develop and take hold. A definite read for all college to career, new or experienced career entrants, no matter the field of interest. No Google search will give you the answers this book can lead you to. Tom shares from the heart in this one of a kind resource combining multiple dimensions of who we are and what we believe, to get us to our next venture."

Denise is Assistant Vice President for Alumni and Career Services at the University of Richmond. Previously she was the Director of the University Career Center at the University of North Carolina at Charlotte for 20 years. She has presented, consulted, and published nationally and internationally (Japan, Germany, and England) in the field as well as participated in television news features on job market and recruiting and dual career family issues in Philadelphia, Dallas, Chicago, and Charlotte.

MONICA MEAGHER

"In gratitude to Tom Bachhuber for beautifully and creatively bringing together the wisdom of his counseling and career development work and the wisdom of his spiritual journey. In doing so, Tom has modeled a method of reflection that draws on listening without (to the expertise and wisdom of others) and listening within (to the promptings of the soul and the voice of God). As a spiritual director, I especially appreciate Tom's dedication to his own interior life and his willingness to share its ebb and flow so openly. Reading TRANSPIRATIONS is like having a spiritual conversation with a beloved friend. It will draw you in, take you deeper and leave you feeling connected. In short, it is an experience of great love for anyone going through a transition."

Monica Meagher is currently serving as Spiritual Director at the Faber Center for Ignatian Spirituality, Marquette University. She is also Regional Director for *Ignatian Volunteer Corps Milwaukee,* providing volunteer and spiritual opportunities for retired adults.

TRANSPIRATIONS

EUGENE F. MERZ, S.J.

"Do not just read this book! Prayerfully ponder it. I was initially overwhelmed by the importance of this project and the wealth of its rich resources; let the creative genius of this effort and its prayerful process work its transformative power upon you!

Tom Bachhuber invites you to take a personal, spiritual, transformative journey with him. No matter where you are on your career or life journey, this book will speak to your mind and heart and guide you through life's inevitable transitions of Endings, Middles and Beginnings.

This book is unique in this way: it provides a rich, personal, vulnerable faith component as its integrating factor. Touched by the wisdom and practicality of Ignatian spirituality, Tom Bachhuber uses personal life experiences, questions and wisdom words to guide and help you reflect on and integrate your own life experiences."

Eugene F. Merz, S.J., a Jesuit priest, has offered spiritual direction and retreats based on the Spiritual Exercises of St. Ignatius and given Ignatian spirituality workshops around the world for laity, priests and religious men and women. He and Carol Ann Smith, SHCJ are the authors of *Moment by Moment: A Retreat in Everyday Life* and *Finding God in Each Moment: The Practice of Discernment in Everyday Life.*

JACK BENNETT

"For when I am weak, then I am strong." (2 Corinthians 12:10) This bedrock of Christian faith has challenged and comforted me throughout my life. Because of Tom Bachhuber's thoughts, writings, and counseling, this staple to a tranquil life has become much clearer. When one grows close to a friend during the formative college years, it makes a lasting impression. Adult life provides the inevitable ups and downs related to family, health, and job challenges. I have been blessed with an "old and new friend" who values wisdom, depth, and the courage of his convictions. Tom's humility and understanding shine brightly in his writing. Tom possesses an uncommon way of looking at the joys and sorrows of life. His insight is grounded in faith, meditation, relationships, and realistic optimism. Tom's very personal approach to professional, individual, and family transitions is inspirational while being practical and spiritual at the same time. The apostle Paul advised us in Romans, 12:12 to: "Rejoice in hope, be patient in tribulation and constant in prayer." Paul provided the blueprint for Tom's masterful look at what is genuinely important in life."

Jack is a highly successful retired high school and college basketball coach, elected to the Wisconsin Basketball Coaches Association Hall of Fame in 2006. As head coach at the University of Wisconsin-Stevens point, he led the Pointers to back to back national championships in 2004 and 2005. He is a frequent speaker throughout the region and takes great pride in integrating his Christian faith into his professional, educational and volunteer work.

KAREN O. DOWD, PH.D.

"I am pleased to provide this endorsement for Dr. Tom Bachhuber's remarkable new book TRANSPIRATIONS: *Guidance for the Head & Heart through Career and Beyond.* In a highly unique approach, Dr. Bachhuber uses his personal experiences with love and loss to help the reader reflect on their own experiences and how these can be used to bring meaning to one's own life in times of personal or career transition.

This book is extremely practical for anyone seeking a new career opportunity, contemplating the next chapter of their life, or going through a major transition, ones' own or that of a good friend or family member. Most career books focus strictly on the techniques of job search and don't deal with the all-important emotional side of facing voluntary or involuntary career transition or making important life decisions.

In TRANSPIRATIONS, Dr. Bachhuber skillfully uses journaling as a vehicle for learning from difficulties we all face in life. He takes a positive view of the curve balls life throws, encouraging the reader to gain strength from losses and mistakes, to be positive when faced with adversity, to learn from challenges. In career/work transitions for example, he has reflections on successful networking, the importance of goal setting, dealing with disappointment, inviting multiple perspectives, tapping into one's personal strengths, and paying attention to non-verbal cues when communicating with employers. These and many other concepts in the book will help anyone who is navigating a difficult work environment, seeking meaningful work, contemplating their next chapter, or helping a friend manage similar challenges."

Dr. Karen Dowd is Assistant Dean, Career Management and Corporate Engagement at the Simon Business School, University of Rochester. She was Executive Director of Career Services and Corporate Engagement for the Daniels College of Business at the University of Denver. She has coauthored two books, *The Ultimate Guide to Getting the Career You Want,* and *Interpersonal Skills in Organizations,* both published by McGraw-Hill.

TRANSPIRATIONS

HONORING A FRIEND

HOWARD E. FIGLER, PH.D.
(1939-2015)

H oward Figler changed the landscape of the career development profession. His writing and speaking influenced thousands of career services professionals in higher education. Through his books: *Path: A Career Workbook for Liberal Arts Students* (Carroll Press); *The Complete Job Search Handbook* (Henry Holt and Company); and *The Career Counselor's Handbook* (with Dick Bolles, Ten Speed Press), he delivered creative insights, ideas and guidance to us as we helped our students.

My personal memories of Howard are rich and varied. There were MAPA memories of morning tennis matches and his dancing to get the band to play longer; a UT visit which included a satisfying run in the heat of an Austin summer, BBQ, Lone Stars, and Tex-Mex feasts; a lazy float down the Delaware with him, his girlfriend du jour and my family; a magical rendezvous at Wimbledon despite the London cold and rain; his kindness to tour my Mom and Dad around the Texas campus during their visit and making good fun of our work using silly words like "krear" and "cruitin"; the privilege of his collaboration on the *Career Waves Newsletter*.

Always, Howard demonstrated a great sense of fun and healthy, self-deprecating humor. His unwavering scorn of career tests, inventories, and assessments as "crutches" which diminished his highest standard for personal career counseling was a cornerstone belief. I treasured his boundless enthusiasm for discussions about best ways to help confused, overwhelmed, and uninspired students.

In thinking hard about his death and the painful loss for all of us, one of Howard's most beautiful qualities was his ability to make other career counselors feel valuable. We all knew Howard thought more deeply and intelligently about our work than anyone. But in professional dialogue, he would listen carefully to us, focusing on the one or two nuggets that we might have uncovered, and paying close attention to just those ideas. He'd skip over the fluff. Then he would ask thoughtful questions which helped us expand and enhance our ideas. And through this caring process, he lifted us to our best selves, where we would feel in partnership with him. This was his gift to us. As I reflect, he always demonstrated the essence of the loving friend and counselor he was. We who were fortunate to know him and thousands who didn't are so grateful for him and his work.

Thank you, Howard.

FOREWORD

TRANSPIRATIONS is unique among life/work planning guides. Most offer prescriptions for dealing with career change and job searches. While often helpful, they usually do not go deep enough to enable the reader to re-examine who they are, what brought them to this point in their lives, and, using the transition, how to re-center their lives with meaning.

Let's face it, life transitions are inevitable. While they may bring excitement about new possibilities and a sense of relief from what was, they also may bring feelings of pain, loss and fear. *TRANSPIRATIONS* tackles the inevitable pains and losses we all experience as part of the human condition but we seldom acknowledge in more than a reactive manner. The book does so by asking us to pause and reflect on psychological and spiritual implications of our current situation so we don't get stuck in negative emotions which can defeat us.

Tom Bachhuber does this gently by describing the significant pains, losses, threats and joys from his own life as examples for us to consider as we face our own transitions.

Among his other competencies, Tom is an expert career counselor. In *TRANSPIRATIONS*, Tom has integrated his extensive experience and knowledge in career counseling with his quest for spiritual understanding. He does so in the narrative tradition and without dogma. He invites you to consider the loss associated with a major life transition, and to use the transition as an opportunity to create new possibilities for a career and life of meaning and contribution. *TRANSPIRATIONS* guides us to go deeper by describing and perhaps realigning our possibilities for the future.

I encourage you to engage this rich book with the fullest of hopes and efforts to secure the important work awaiting you.

Sincerely,

Bill Banis

William Banis, Ph.D. is the retired Vice President of Student Affairs at Northwestern University, serving for eleven years. He is the former director of career services at Northwestern, Old Dominion University and Hartford University.

He has been a National Certified Counselor (NCC) and National Certified Career Counselor (NCCC), counseling more than 4,000 clients. He was inducted into the Academy of Fellows by the National Association of Colleges and Employers in 1999 for his contributions to the career services and human resources professions and was recognized as a Pillar of the Profession in 2011 by the *National Association of Student Personnel Administrators.*

TABLE OF CONTENTS

DEDICATION III

IN APPRECIATION V

PRAISE FOR TRANSPIRATIONS IX

HONORING A FRIEND XXI

FOREWORD XXIII

INTRODUCTION 1

CHAPTER 1: ENDINGS 13

  1. Seeds Of Hope 15

  2. Transitions Come In Many Forms 19

  3. Keep On Keeping On 23

  4. Waiting And Questioning 27

  5. Facing Fear With An Action 31

  6. It's About Love 35

  7. Moving Forward With Structure 39

  8. Knowing You Will Be OK 43

  9. Overcoming The Status Quo 47

  10. Your Fears Are Not You 51

  11. Turning To God 55

  12. Acting On Fear 59

  13. Preparing, Listening, Respecting 63

  14. Making The Right Move 67

  15. Doing More With Less 71

CHAPTER 2: MIDDLES   75

1. Thankful For Pieces Of Light.................................77

2. Seeing The Deeper Things 83

3. We Know More Than We Think 87

4. Resting Before Proceeding 91

5. Like A Moon Rising 97

6. Different Perspectives Matter 101

7. I Had Hoped It Would Be Different 105

8. Doing It Yourself And With Others 111

9. Your Best Conversation Is Needed: Lessons From Helen Ann 115

10. Gifts Are To Be Discovered 119

11. There's Hope In Preparation 123

12. Finding The Silver Lining 127

13. Getting On With It Inspires 131

14. Light In Darkness 135

15. Words Can Be Overrated 139

16. Finding God In The Foxhole 143

CHAPTER 3: BEGINNINGS   147

1. Honesty Is The Best Policy............................149

2. Managing Expectations 153

3. Finding Our Spirit 157

4. Going Deeper As We Begin Anew 161

5. Taking In Love 165

6. Being Grateful 171

7. Patience Is Not Just A Virtue 177

8. And So We're Back To Love 181

9. Counting On What's Real 187

10. The Truth Of The Work 191

11. New Perspectives Help 197

12. Heaven On Earth 201

13. Everything's Changed 207

CHAPTER 4: IGNATIAN SPIRITUALITY   213

Ignatius: A Brief Biography 215

Bringing Together Elements of Ignatian Spirituality and Transition . . .219

(1) Spirituality & Faith. 221

(2) Vocation. 225

(3) Decision-making/Discernment 231

(4) Action Toward Work/Service. 237

EPILOGUE   253

APPENDICES   259

Prayer at the Beginning of LifeSHIFT:
Work & the Christian Journey Retreats .260

Transitions 261

A Poem About the Soul. 262

Disappointment 265

Lord, I Have Time 267

Patient Trust 269

A Poem On Dreaming. 270

Who Am I? 271

For a New Beginning. 273

God of My Life 274

Starlings in Winter. 275

Making Successful Career/Work Transitions
Twenty-two Random Ideas* 277

BIBLIOGRAPHY   287

INDEX   293

ABOUT THE AUTHOR   301

INTRODUCTION

TRANSPIRATIONS—"Now that's a curious word," you're thinking as you peek into this book. My friend Yesh encouraged me to use it; we brainstormed titles for my newsletter and agreed that a combination of "transition," "inspiration" and "spirituality" described my messages. We made up the word, so imagine our surprise when we learned that it actually means "the nourishing flow of water and nutrients through plants." Nice.

Writing has always been a more personal and easier way of sharing my ideas and deeper feelings. I was a letter writer before email, texting and social media dominated communications. When I helped start The Center for Life Transitions, I knew we would have a newsletter—I had written them for multiple organizations.

I first began journaling in 1998 as part of an initial year at a school called *KAIROS: School for Spiritual Formation,* started by the Mennonites in eastern Pennsylvania and open to all faiths. Kairos is Greek for God's time, different from chronos meaning earthly time. We assembled one weekend a month at the wonderful Jesuit Center in Wernersville, PA, for prayer, study, discussion and solitude. I treasured the time and place.

Upon entering the gates my first weekend, I felt like I had returned home—a sentiment many first-time retreatants express. Walking the halls of the spacious English Renaissance building, I experienced a fresh presence of God in my life. I lingered at each statue, painting, tapestry and relic. I later concluded it was not because of the architecture, holy memorabilia or church-related articles but rather because of the spirits of the countless people over decades who shared their hearts with God and each other there.

INSPIRATION FOR WRITING

One of our *KAIROS* resources was a sweet little book entitled, *The Little Monk,* by Harry Farra, about a young man's monastic progress from novice to abbot. I loved the book but was particularly affected by the chapter on journaling. The little monk called his journal his fourth counselor—the church, friends and prayer being the other three. He told how his writings evolved into a time machine, as they allowed him to see where God was and wasn't. I liked that idea. I found my lined notebooks to be a useful tool in my spiritual journey.

I sketched and scrawled events, activities, moods of all kinds—personal, emotional, family, career and faith related. I never hesitated to show my true feelings to God, often being angry over the state of the world, personal frustrations, disappointments and, most easily, problems encountered by my children. One time my daughter was in a dirt bike accident and broke her arm in several places. "Enough already, God," I wrote in big letters. I didn't directly blame God but that never stopped me from getting angry. I got in the habit of writing my life— the exciting (to me), sorrowful and mundane. It seemed natural to record my feelings, fears and triumphs as I encountered life difficulties as well as the joyful events.

ESSENCE OF THIS BOOK, TRANSPIRATIONS

I've chosen to focus on five major events in my life—my dad's death (2005), my open heart surgery (2006), my cancer diagnosis/treatment (2011), my mom's death (2015) and the birth of Oona Mae, my wife's and my first grandchild (2016). I've collected a variety of journal writings from my TRANSPIRATIONS newsletter during these times in trying to show their relationship to issues people face in work-related transitions, e.g., job hunting, career or ministry change, and retirement. The excerpts from my dad's death and Oona Mae's birth are few, as they became an important addition once the book was started.

It may seem peculiar to connect ideas from personal health, death and birth to those of career/retirement, but the emotions and work required for fulfillment are the same. I like William Bridges' (author of multiple books and perhaps the most recognized authority on transition) distinction between change and transition. Change is what happens to us while transition is how we internally adjust and adapt so we can continue moving ahead.

In all cases, we must address our emotions and accomplish tasks as we strive to move forward.

THE SPIRITUAL SIDE OF TRANSITIONS

My life and work have always included spirituality. I grew up Catholic and had great respect for the smart, engaging nuns who taught me in grade school. As I aged, faith, spirituality and God became a combination of curiosity, inner guidance and complex mystery. I had and have very few definitive answers; mostly questions. But I believe in a God who connects to us in ways which can be personal, strengthening and inspiring. I'm also quick to tell people that my favorite Gospel story is about the father who brings his epileptic son into a crowded marketplace to seek healing from Jesus. The father's honest and vulnerable reply to Jesus' question about his faith is, "Lord, I believe. Help me with my unbelief." I so admire this father for his courage in this instance where the health of his son is on the line. In front of everyone. And I resonate to Jesus' respect for the father's honesty as he heals the boy (Mark 9:15-29).

My work with individuals and groups over the years has often addressed faith and spiritual questions. Thomas Merton, Henri Nouwen, Parker Palmer, Mary Oliver, Oswald Chambers and Joyce Rupp were my mainstays for content and quotes. But when Gene Merz, S.J. gave me a copy of his book (Moment by Moment) and introduced me to Ignatius of Loyola, founder of the Jesuits, another phase of my spiritual journey began. And later, my friend Monica provided an Ignatian quote which summarized my work philosophy. It brought career development and spirituality into one eloquent statement for me.

"There are very few people who realize what God would make of them…if they abandoned themselves into God's hands, and let themselves be formed by Grace. In calling me to live my special qualities and characteristics, God planted deep in myself an original purpose, what my concrete self adds up to and to live that out."

In his Spiritual Exercises, Ignatius had something to say about the emotions, feelings and thoughts we have in life transitions. He called them "motions of the soul" defined as "consolations" and "desolations." We feel God's presence in consolation; our outlook is positive, strong and encouraged. Other feelings may include hope, joy, community, purpose, direction, and connection to God as Creator, Source, Guide.

Desolation is the opposite as we feel discouraged, fearful, lonely and weak. For me, God is at a distance. In each case, Ignatius advises that these "motions" flow in and out of our interior lives. Like Bridges, he used the language of "beginnings," "middle" and "endings" to guide us in determining where these "motions" are leading us in transition.

FROM RULE 5
PARAPHRASED FROM HIS SPIRITUAL EXERCISES

"We ought to pay close attention to the progression of thoughts (motions). If the beginning, middle, and end of it are altogether good and tend entirely to what is right, that is a sign of God's influence i.e. consolation. It is, however, a clear sign that the line of thought originates from the influence of desolation, the enemy of our spiritual progress, if thoughts distract or disquiet us from what we had previously proposed to do.

A central tenet of Ignatian Spirituality is "magis"—Latin for more or "the greater good" and is from the phrase, "Ad majorem Dei gloriam"— for the greater glory of God. Ignatius believed that we should strive for this goal in everything we do. And that God can be discovered and engaged in all aspects of our lives to guide and strengthen us.

THE BRIDGES WAY FOR
UNDERSTANDING TRANSITIONS AND USING THIS BOOK

As you view the model on the next page, you will see how William Bridges' ideas are helpful in many ways. He divides the transition process into three phases: 1. **Endings**, 2. **Middles** (Bridges calls it the Neutral Zone) and 3. **Beginnings**. Each phase has its inherent emotions to address and tasks to accomplish for making a successful transition. You'll see there are headings of **Emotions**, and **Key Tasks** as well as **Spiritual Questions** and an **Ignatian Reflection** in the model. These statements, questions and reflections may help you better understand your transition as well as move forward toward new, meaningful work. Additionally, you may want to use the model as a means for managing your selection and use of the writings in the book. The book is divided into three chapters, **Chapter One—Endings**, **Chapter Two— Middles** and **Chapter Three—Beginnings**, corresponding to the model.

CENTER FOR LIFE TRANSITIONS
CenterForLifeTransitions.net

MANAGING WORK TRANSITIONS *

STAGE	EMOTIONS	KEY TASKS	SPIRITUAL QUESTIONS	IGNATIAN REFLECTIONS **
ENDINGS	Grief over losing what was comfortable, good and/or meaningful. Regret. Anger. Anxiety. Self-doubt. Denial. Lethargy. Fear and even depression.	Gain support and help. Identify significant personal, work and spiritual resources. Engage in positive self-talk and don't allow myths and misinformation to discourage me. Believe in myself, in my field and in my work.	How can I remain or return to a positive outlook, believing in myself, my support system/resources and God in order to have the strength, wisdom and love to move forward?	How can I gather the graces (lessons, kindnesses, gifts) received before and during this time and take even a small step toward discovering what might be ahead?
MIDDLES	Confusion and uncertainty over the future. Skepticism. Ambivalence over the work required. Frustration over failed strategies. Feeling stuck. Hope begins as some progress can be seen or imagined.	Commit to exploration and deep research of organizations/ opportunities. Engage key people in my field for direction, support, ideas, referrals i.e. true networking. Achieve balance between using web and personal resources.	What will I do to reassure myself that hope is alive; that what I'm doing and how I'm praying will continue to be meaningful?	In my uncertainty, immobility or beginning progress, can I get in touch with my longing for magis (greater good) that God and I desire in my work, communicating how my gifts (concrete self) can contribute to others, organizations and the world?
BEGINNINGS	Excitement. Anticipation. Relief. Gratitude. Feeling confident in applying lessons learned to new tasks and work environment.	Demonstrate gratefulness to people who help me. Advance in my work and workplace with confidence, caution and preparation for the next transition. Continue to meet with people in my field.	How do I best acknowledge, respect and celebrate my "reinvented self" in this new work, while continuing preparations and prayers for transitions ahead?	In getting close to or actually living my new work, can my heart and dispositions be open to generosity, trust and hope, so my faith can grow in love?

* Model is inspired by the work of William Bridges; Narrative by Tom Bachhuber.

* "There are very few people who realize what God would make of them...if they abandoned themselves into God's hands and let themselves be formed by Grace. In calling me to live my special qualities and characteristics, God planted deep in me an original purpose, what my concrete self adds up to and to live that out." - Ignatius of Loyola

Using the Bridges categories, each selection is titled and begins with an entry entitled **Tom's Journal** about one of the five events mentioned earlier—1. my Dad's death, 2. my heart surgery, 3. my cancer diagnosis/treatment, 4. my Mom's death and 5. the birth of my wife's and my granddaughter. The excerpts from these journal entries are not in chronological order within each chapter. What happened is important and not when it happened. There is a symbol which identifies each event.

**AT THE END
WITH DAD**

**HEART
HEALING**

**A CANCER
JOURNEY**

**MOM'S
DYING**

**THE MIRACLE
OF OONA**

Following the journal entries, work-related ideas, information and teachings appear under the title, **Reflections For Work.** This information will vary in application to your career, work, job search or retirement situation.

The content from both the **Journal** excerpts and **Reflections For Work** focus on aspects of **Emotions, Key Tasks, Spiritual**

Questions and **Ignatian Reflections** highlighted at the beginning of each chapter, endings, middles and beginnings. There will be overlap and in cases, there is material in one chapter which could go in another. Emotions, tasks, questions and reflections may be applicable to all three stages of transition.

The **Ponder** part of each writing includes questions and observations related to the topic. The final element **What's the "Next Thing" You Will Do?** is founded in WWI chaplain Oswald Chambers' teaching that when we are confused or confounded, it's because we have partial visions. We need to stop, reflect, pray and do the "next thing." We'll know what that "next thing" is.

Successful transitions are a series of "next things." I hope you'll be inspired to use the lines behind **Ponder** and **What's the "Next Thing "You Will Do?** for note taking and journaling.

THE WORK OF MAKING A SUCCESSFUL TRANSITION

I have faith that you will see the connections between my experiences and the work necessary for your successful job, ministry, career and/or retirement transition. And that these connections will provide renewed energy and commitment for your journey.

The effort we need to make in moving toward success is the same for all kinds of transitions:

❖ Reflect with intentionality and depth about yourself—your skills, your values, your gifts, your relationships, your God;

❖ Review existing resources and discover new ones (print, places, people, technology, media) for help;

❖ Explore and research with courage work opportunities and possibilities using print, technology and people;

❖ Clarify objectives or goals which inspire you to become the person you long to be or attain the work which will add new meaning to your life. Articulate them in writing;

❖ Take action (researching organizations, networking, developing personal marketing resources/tools, secure meetings/interviews, follow-up) towards achieving those objectives;

❖ Integrate prayer, guidance from others and fluid, adaptable plans into the transition process.

YOU MAY FIND THE THIS BOOK HELPFUL IF YOU ARE:

❖ Approaching or experiencing retirement and searching for new meaning in the next work/life phase;

❖ Experiencing dissatisfaction with your career/work/ministry and looking for fresh perspectives and purpose;

❖ Feeling unhappy in your work or career and looking for a change or new direction;

❖ Desiring to look inward and use spiritual ideas/resources to help with discernment;

❖ Needing encouragement, inspiration and a closer relationship between your transition work and your faith/spiritual life;

❖ Going through a challenging time physically, emotionally and/or spiritually.

My hope is that TRANSPIRATIONS will help you with the journey that is this "wild and precious life" (as Mary Oliver says in her poem, *A Summer Day*) allowing you to see new connections to your deeper self—the place where your God-given talents and previously undiscovered strength and inspiration reside. By tapping into this place, you will quite possibly see that God is there and, as this Source, you will find guidance and support toward your next work objective.

USING THIS BOOK IN DIFFERENT WAYS

The book you are reviewing or holding can be read straight through as any self-help, spiritual, career or job search book. It can also be used as a daily resource as you move through the work transition process. Divided into three parts of **Endings**, **Middles** and **Beginnings**, you may want to determine where you are in your transition and select the corresponding chapter of the book as your starting place. Begin there and proceed sequentially or randomly through the chapter.

As a daily guide, you may want to browse the book, turning to the individual reading which seems most useful for that day or situation. Use the **Contents** each time you open the book, reading each title and choosing one that seems to match your circumstances and needs. It could be in any chapter and may not necessarily connect to the part of a transition you're presently in. Let your intuition or deeper self choose.

As you engage the challenges of making a successful transition, it is important to set your sights high. Theresa of Avila is a role model for us. As founder of the Carmelite order, she was a scholar, writer, executive and mystic. Her lifetime work involved several transitions and her poetic words inspire:

"It is a great help in our quest to have high aspirations, because often our actions begin with our thoughts and our dreams. It is not pride to have great desires.

Like the saints we need to be humble but bold in our pursuit, trusting God and not ourselves. For our Lord loves and seeks courageous souls.

Let us not fail to reach our destiny because we have been too timid; too cautious in our desires, because we sought too little.

It is true that I might stumble for trying to do too much too soon, but it is certain that I will never succeed if I hope for too little or, out of fear of failing, start not at all."

My prayer for you is a meaningful and inspired start. Good things will surely follow.

Tom

TRANSPIRATIONS

CHAPTER ONE

ENDINGS

ENDINGS
ENDINGS

STAGE
ENDINGS

EMOTIONS
Grief over losing what was comfortable, good and/or meaningful. Regret. Anger. Anxiety. Self-doubt. Denial. Lethargy. Fear and even depression.

KEY TASKS
Gain support and help. Identify significant personal, work and spiritual resources. Engage in positive self-talk and don't allow myths and misinformation to discourage me. Believe in myself, in my field and in my work.

SPIRITUAL QUESTIONS
How can I remain or return to a positive outlook, believing in myself, my support system/resources and God in order to have the strength, wisdom and love to move forward?

IGNATIAN REFLECTIONS **
How can I gather the graces (lessons, kindnesses, gifts) received before and during this time and take even a small step toward discovering what might be ahead?

NOTES

Tom's Journal: Heart Healing
1. SEEDS OF HOPE

...and so the good Doctor G looked at me squarely and spoke these difficult to hear words, "You need a new valve." While I sat stunned, I mused, "In my car?" He discussed the need for open heart surgery to replace my existing aortic valve, explaining that I had been born (and had lived almost 60 years) with a bicuspid valve (two cusps or openings instead of the requisite three), and now this valve I had happily ignored but counted on all these years, was failing.

I was blindsided, being an athlete my whole life. Yesterday I ran 6 miles. This protest was quickly brought short, however, by the expert's words, "Sometimes, the first symptom of this condition is a fatal heart attack." He had my attention.

And so a week later, I sit in the big blue chair overlooking our snow- covered backyard, observing the hawthorn tree with its white-capped frozen berries, strangely calm, and feeling inspired to move ahead with more purpose in my life.

REFLECTIONS FOR WORK

William Bridges says the "endings" can be full of shock, grief, fear, anger and denial but as acceptance settles in, you move ahead. When acceptance happens on a substantive level, good things take place. Eckhart Tolle believes this acceptance takes us away from negativism to a place he calls "true Being." When that happens, possibilities for growth, e.g. meaningful work, are limitless. And the energy, resources and spirit to carry out a successful transition can be realized.

As we slowly move from acceptance to the confusion, complexity and sometimes immobility which follows, there is a need to find strength. Paula D'Arcy in her Lenten publication, *Daybreaks*, writes, "...there is a truer nature within me...a true self. This nature precedes my birth and isn't bound by emotions, body or mind. It is clear and free, the same substance as God—the same essence as love." I believe it is this "essence of love" which helps move us forward from crisis and uncertainty to a place of confidence and hope.

Whether facing job loss early in a career, mid-life career confusion or consternation over defining meaningful volunteer work in retirement, we need to begin by accepting where we are. With this acceptance will come the gradual realization that there are inner and outer resources which can help us gain new direction. Find meaningful work. Knowing we are loved by the people around us is key and amazing energy can flow into transition activity resulting in success.

PONDER

What do you have to do in this "endings" part of your transition in order to get to that place of acceptance? And then move from immobility to action.

_____

_____

_____

Reflect on the shock you felt when a change at work blindsided you. Stew on it all you want but try hard to not let it overwhelm you.

_____

_____

_____

Where can your "true Being" which contains God's love be found and how will it move you forward?

_____

_____

_____

WHAT'S THE "NEXT THING" YOU WILL DO?

_____

_____

_____

_____

Tom's Journal: A Cancer Journey
2. TRANSITIONS COME IN MANY FORMS

It's finally clear. After getting my cardiologist's report on my heart's 'greatness' four years after open heart surgery, the radiologist says I have some lymph nodes larger than he likes and I should see my doc. Great. Three months later and having gone about my business of living and working under the cloud of uncertainty, we now know it's grade 1, slow growing, non-Hodgkin's follicular lymphoma—stage 3 as located in three places. And that's cancer for the uninitiated. Not in the bone marrow. Good. No real symptoms. Good. Dr. F. says it's the kind of cancer you usually die with...not from. Good. Has kind of an optimistic tone to it. Time to go to work and get it into remission and continue to "remiss it" so I can add 15-20 or more years to my life. I'm already 64— so 80 plus or so feels pretty good.

REFLECTIONS FOR WORK

Change happens in all aspects of our lives. We get that but often struggle in managing these changes. They take an emotional and often a physical toll. However, the resilience we develop in responding to change in one transition may help us in another.

This is the first journal entry I made after receiving the diagnosis of my new disease. I've journaled for "self-therapy" for many years, but with this diagnosis it took on new importance. I've never shied away from my mortality but now it's more real, closer. Writing helps.

William Bridges tells us we must grieve loss in the first stage of transition, "endings." I still felt healthy with this diagnosis so there was no loss for me there. Nothing to grieve. But perhaps my loss was the confidence I had throughout my life that my pace toward death was comfortably slow. After the diagnosis, not so much. The uncertainty of my health and the knowledge that there were new challenges ahead in a seemingly shortened life unfolded together. My wife Leslie put it well– I lost the comfort of vagueness which allows most of us to keep the disquieting knowledge of our own mortality at bay. For me, talking to loved ones and writing about my feelings in this situation was part of that grieving process.

I believe this is true for job changes as well. We need to acknowledge both our grief and our anger in job loss. Even a voluntary job change involves loss. It can be helpful to write and talk about the qualities of the work and workplace which we will miss. Maybe we also need to come to grips with myths we believed about that job, e.g. "this work will always be satisfying or was perfect" or "my job is too important for them to let me go." Finding language for our sadness, confusion or anger allows us to discover the energy we need for the work ahead. Getting that next job—a good one, which has meaning and promise.

PONDER

Reflect on the external changes that are causing your internal transition.

_____

_____

_____

_____

What do you need to do in order to grieve what you miss so that you can move toward new, meaningful work?

_____

_____

WHAT'S THE "NEXT THING" YOU WILL DO?

_____

_____

_____

_____

NOTES

Tom's Journal: A Cancer Journey
3. KEEP ON KEEPING ON

Before the diagnosis, the thing I felt best about during the early time of uncertainty in cancer testing was my willingness to "keep living." This may sound trite as what else can you do? But for me, it was meaningful as I continued to engage people in work and play–little activities and big ones too like the wedding of my daughter, in ways which felt authentic. I laughed, listened, cared and spoke with enthusiasm. Spirit. Sometimes it wasn't easy.

As I reflect back, it was this daily living that nourished me with the love I needed to be less fearful and embrace each day. Additional journal entries reflect on giving and receiving love in my spiritual life too.

And I think I was able to do this because of the work I've done over time on my faith. Not faith in some glorious Disneyland afterlife but the deeper understanding gained through life's ups and downs, trials and travails; the larger wisdom which fosters hope and provides a connection to something bigger; a God who is real; certainly mysterious, often perplexing and confounding, but personal and able to receive and give love. I believe this.

REFLECTIONS FOR WORK

In William Bridges' first stage named "endings," anxiety and anger can be significant. It can stop us in our tracks—paralyze us.

The time of disempowerment for me was after I was told by the radiologist to see an oncologist about the scan results. This was an area of medicine about which I knew little and would have been happy to continue knowing less. I went through the paces of further testing and discussions over a two-month period, waking up each morning with the pain of uncertainty in my gut. I kept everything pretty much inside, sharing only minimally with my wife until I knew the cancer was real. I tried to live each day fully. Life was still good, but certainly different, as I waited for news. My writing reflected this tension between hope and despair.

In the muck of a work transition before a clear career direction is gained, there is a tendency to close down. Get selfish. Feel sorry for ourselves. Eckhart Tolle teaches about the danger of self-defeating messages like "Nobody really understands what I'm going through," "I'll never find a good job," and "I need to be emotionally separated from my loved ones as I work this out." He calls these messages "phantoms." We must fight these phantoms by denying their existence. Daily living can nurture us. Important energy can be found in the people around us. Hope resides there and it's hope we need the most during these times.

It is a big challenge to produce at work when you know change is coming. Hard to live and work in the present when the future is uncertain. Equally so when things are going south in job hunting. Resumes aren't getting answered. Interviews not materializing. You may have to search that spiritual part of yourself for strength to continue. And turn to the deeper friends and colleagues for support.

Because continuing is what it's all about. As you persist even with the smallest of gains, you'll take pride in that progress. Courage is what you're demonstrating to secure the success you deserve. And will find.

PONDER

Reflect on the people and aspects of your daily life which you have been missing because you're disengaged, focused too much on your own worries.

_____

_____

What self-defeating statements have you been making to yourself?

_____

_____

What can you do about it and how might this help you find hope?

_____

_____

WHAT'S THE "NEXT THING" YOU WILL DO?

_____

_____

_____

_____

NOTES

Tom's Journal: Mom's Dying

4. WAITING AND QUESTIONING

Mom is clearly not the Mom I want to see today. Her eyes have no sparkle, her smile is weak and she seems to have little interest in life as we know it. She hasn't had much sight or hearing and has been wheelchair bound for over two years—who can blame her for turning inward? It's times like these that I wonder why she is still here. I recall my Grandma dying and telling me she didn't know why she was still here. My stammering reply was something about teaching her family patience and dignity. Doesn't seem very helpful now.

We just finished a painful 20 minutes with the well-meaning but inept visiting priest. He asked to give Mom the "Final" Anointment. She was anointed a week ago. Guess he gets to check it off again. Mom was barely cognizant but peaceful. At the end, he closed with the Lord's Prayer and Mom perked up—she wanted to pray it with him. But to my dismay, he wouldn't slow down to pray at her pace. He raced to the conclusion with Mom's words trailing behind—and her furrowed brow painfully visible. He left with a cursory blessing and perfunctory goodbye. I'll never forgive myself for not interrupting him and asking him to begin the prayer again, allowing my Mom to say it with him.

REFLECTIONS FOR WORK

Effective group leaders know how to gain valuable input from those who are less verbal or too shy to speak in groups. These quieter folks have ideas that are valuable and their participation is critical to success. Getting their thoughts requires sensitivity, patience and more time than many leaders are willing to give. A shame. Deeper listening and sensitive, but direct questions usually leads to richer discussions from both confident and shy participants.

As a coach, I sometimes make an error in rushing to dispense my "wisdom" on a work transition issue or dilemma instead of waiting for more insights from the person. Networking can be like that. We so desperately want to say the right thing and say it well that we forget that a great question is absolutely the best way to make a powerful impact. A thoughtful question is poignant—it demonstrates your authentic concern for the person. It becomes that all-important building block toward your credibility and eventual exposure to opportunity or referral.

Joe Sweeney in his book, *Networking is a Contact Sport,* emphasizes the giving aspect of a networking discussion— we are there to give not just get. What can we give, you may ask? Our time, interest and thoughtful questions are incredible gifts in these encounters.

NETWORKEE (PERSON WITH KNOWLEDGE, POWER AND CONTACTS YOU WANT)

"We've just installed a new technology in order to increase production in our packaging department. It's been three months and we're not pleased with the quarterly report."

NETWORKER

"Oh, we've had that new technology for two years now and have never had any problems—we're staying the course."

STRONGER NETWORKER

"That's disappointing—what kinds of analyses have you been doing? We just completed a study and unfortunately didn't track operator training and experience adequately. How would you feel about a meeting where we could address our common challenges?"

Waiting, questioning and not rushing to judgement or action is valuable during this ending phase of transition.

PONDER

Write down situations where in retrospect, you wished you could have been more patient or listened more carefully.

_____

_____

_____

What causes you at times to speak too much, interrupt someone, or push the conversation at a faster pace?

_____

_____

_____

Imagine a conversation which may occur when you are networking and note how you might be more sensitive to the person you're with—and how you might better learn about his/her situation.

_____

_____

_____

_____

Write down questions you will ask. Ensure they are specific and based in research about your contact, organization and work you're exploring.

_____

_____

_____

_____

WHAT'S THE "NEXT THING" YOU WILL DO?

_____

_____

_____

_____

Tom's Journal: Heart Healing
5. FACING FEAR WITH AN ACTION

I ponder these tests which will tell me if I need my heart renewed with a new aortic valve. If I have to go through this, my life will be changed, certainly. Maybe for the best, I reflect. Good things even great things can come from adversity. Maybe I'll see my future more clearly. Priorities will be determined. The doc says I'll have 20 plus years before my heart will give out—maybe longer as new things develop. That sounds encouraging.

I think I've had three tests in the past month. It's curious as I lie waiting for new pictures of my heart, I continue to be calm. Why? God is somehow connected here. I reflect on Psalms 23 and 42, my favorites for many years.

"He leadeth me by still waters; he restores my soul." [23]

"Deep calls to deep in the roar of your waterfalls; all your waves and breakers have swept over me." [42]

REFLECTIONS FOR WORK

Paula D'Arcy helps us understand fear: "I was witnessing the nature of fear. Gripped by fear, I've sometimes stayed in dim rooms and dark corners—like clinging to transitions that have bound me and have fallen into patterns that brought no joy. I never saw as I wandered in those dark and lonely spaces, that freedom was one step away, or that the Spirit could lead me to larger places."

Sometimes we have to trust our spirit as we face challenges. When we do, we find ourselves acting in different ways—maybe more effective ways. We find the mentor we've been missing. Maybe we prepare for the critical meeting with our boss with more rigor or reach out to new leadership in our profession through a networking meeting we wouldn't have otherwise tried to schedule. Possibly we decide to step back and take time to rest before moving on to the next job. At times, doing even simple things like adding a recommendation to our LinkedIn profile or making a single improvement to our resume can give us a spark of courage. Opportunities from this adversity are many! Working on little things can help you see them.

PONDER

How do you stay calm in crises at work?

What's the silver lining as you're viewing this change in job, career or retirement?

_____

_____

_____

_____

What are the means you have to access the Spirit and free yourself from "the dark and lonely places" you may be in?

_____

_____

_____

_____

WHAT'S THE "NEXT THING" YOU WILL DO?

_____

_____

_____

_____

NOTES

Tom's Journal: A Cancer Journey
6. IT'S ABOUT LOVE

The tech calls my name and says, "Hi, I'm Ann and I'm here to take care of you." We walk like old friends to the chemo room as I verify the spelling of my name and date of birth. I get a room with a view of budding pear trees on a breeze-blown pond. Sweet.

No matter what the scan shows in my meeting tomorrow with the good Doctor F, most of my life will continue as it is—rich and full. So Thomas, don't lose heart. Regardless of what these nasty cells are doing or how many are still hanging around, you will continue to fight; your work, play and prayer will not stop. Your God is not going anywhere; Les loves you and is by your side. Hope springs eternal. Love is hanging around.

I lay in the PET scan tube getting pictures taken of my insides and while soft music played, I felt like I was in heaven. There were clouds and sky painted on the ceiling overhead. Tears came as I re-flected on how blessed my life has been and is. How from the very beginning, I have had loving people around me. I thought of my par-ents, brothers, cousins, teachers, coaches, bosses, friends, colleagues, Les and our kids— so, so many blessings. And while in that tube, my heart sang. I wanted the time to last longer.

REFLECTIONS FOR WORK

The Beatles hit "All You Need Is Love" always came off a bit corny to me. Sure, love is great but we need a lot of other things as we seek to successfully move through transitions. Like courage, resilience, hope, and good timing. Luck.

How do you define love anyway? The Greeks looked at it in four different ways—family, friendship, romance and divine. We know love when we see it, but it is hard to describe. A true emotion of affection and attraction? Feelings of kindness and care followed by action? All or some of this? The apostle Paul provides a beautiful and most useful definition in 1 Corinthians 13:4-7.

> *Love is patient, love is kind. It does not envy, it does not boast, it is not proud. It does not dishonor others, it is not self-seeking, it is not easily angered, it keeps no record of wrongs. Love does not delight in evil but rejoices with the truth. It always protects, always trusts, always hopes, always perseveres.*

As I reflect on the previous year, it is love however defined which has kept me going. People have loved me throughout this experience —and in an assortment of ways.

Henri Nouwen in his book, *The Inner Voice of Love*, writes about how "taking in love" is what's critical when we're feeling disempowered.

Our tendency is to work harder or try a new strategy. I've advised people countless times that when things aren't working and you're discouraged, try something new. Take bigger risks. Maybe that's not the most helpful.

Henri encourages us "to take something in that deepens and strengthens our sense of goodness and allows our inaction, blockage or pain to be embraced by love." Then and only then will we gain the strength we need to move forward. The more we come to know ourselves— spirit, mind and body—as truly loved, the more free we are to be our true selves, and find that meaningful work which is ours. So, sometimes it's not about enhancing your job seeking attitude or activities but rather reflecting on the love in your life.

PONDER

How can you more fully realize how much you are loved by the people in your life?

_____

_____

_____

Make a list of these people and how they love you.

_____

_____

_____

_____

How can this love strengthen you to make future decisions and take the important steps necessary for success in your transition?

_____

_____

_____

_____

How do you identify God's love and how does it come into this transition?

_____

_____

_____

_____

WHAT'S THE "NEXT THING" YOU WILL DO?

_____

_____

_____

_____

Tom's Journal: Heart Healing

7. MOVING FORWARD WITH STRUCTURE

I lie on the examination table waiting for the doctor to come and gently, I hope, ease a tube down my throat as part of a TEE (Trans Esophageal Echocardiogram) test. The procedure will provide information about my weakened valve and resulting aneurysm at the base of the aorta. Information that is critical to the corrective surgery. I'm anxious so I attempt to meditate—breathing slowly, deeply and reflecting on how this procedure is good and important. I go through a litany of the blessings in my life; grateful for people who love me and the professionalism of those taking care of me at this moment. I feel better thinking about all the people in my corner—and the steps I'm taking to get this situation resolved. A peacefulness descends; I smile. This will work out.

REFLECTIONS FOR WORK

I've found that my coaching clients gain new strength and inspiration in their transition work when they complete a "Personal Assets Worksheet" identifying not only their central gifts—where interests, skills and passions intersect—but the important people in their network and how they can help. Part of this process is affirming the truth that people who care about us truly want to help—and will do extraordinary things for us.

Mary Heppner's *Career Transition Inventory* measuring "Readiness, Confidence, Personal Control, Support and Independence" is also a useful tool. Coach/counselor and client find practical language to describe the inner resources and challenges in securing new, meaningful work. Good things happen when we take the time to assess the things we have going for us. And taking this action can inspire us as we get more involved in the transition process.

PONDER

What kind of structure and support would be most valuable right now in giving you the positive outlook you need to be successful in the next step of your transition work?

_____

_____

_____

_____

Who are the people you can count on? How will you communicate with them?

_____

_____

_____

_____

Why are you waiting to contact them for help?

_____

_____

_____

_____

WHAT'S THE "NEXT THING" YOU WILL DO?

_____

_____

_____

_____

NOTES

Tom's Journal: Heart Healing
8. KNOWING YOU WILL BE OK

I sit in the blue chair and read a bit about Gnostic faith in the "The Nag Hamaradi Scriptures" given to me by my son, Jay. "Western civilization is rooted in three impulses—reason, faith and gnosis" (inner knowing). I particularly like that last one. There is a part of us which "knows"—just because it does.

Gnosis must relate to the soul. I reflect on those quiet, quickly passing moments when I just know God is there; like when I've faced those tests which will tell me if I need open heart surgery or not. God is in it. Whether I need surgery or not doesn't seem to be the issue. I recall my Dad telling me about his "kitchen experience" the night before his heart surgery. As he felt God's presence, a great sense of relief and calm, even joy and it had nothing to do with whether he lived or died from the operation.

I like the Gnostic writings of Phillip, Thomas, Mary and others. These holy people had unique relationships with Jesus, based on both actions and their unspoken inner knowing. From "The Gospel of Thomas"—"Teacher, my mouth is utterly unable to say what you are like." And Jesus said, "Thomas, I shall give you what no eye has seen, what no ear has heard, what no hand has touched; what has not risen in the human heart." I believe we each have this gift—this unseen, unheard and untouched "strength" for lack of a better word. And we all need it when times are difficult.

REFLECTIONS FOR WORK

When have you faced adversity and somehow, you just knew you were going to be alright? Maybe it was before a big meeting or presentation. Or preparing for a conversation with your boss where you had to convince him or her that a program you headed was successful. Or even a discussion when you knew you were losing your position. Sometimes you just know that a job is not right for you.

Part of your confidence was probably based on thorough preparation. You did all the right things beforehand, e.g., accomplished thorough research; compiled evidence with bulleted points at your fingertips; and prepared cogent, concise arguments. Confidence results from this preparation. But there was more. "Inner knowing" sometimes just manifests itself. Call it strength or maybe grace. Maybe chalk it up to years of working and praying your faith. It's the fruit of your labors. And it makes all the difference in facing challenges. No matter what happens, you will be alright.

PONDER

What are the ways you can prepare for adversity?

_____

_____

_____

_____

Think of an adversity or challenge you have conquered. How much was due to your preparation? And how much was because of something deeper and less understood?

_____

_____

_____

_____

What are you presently doing in your spiritual life to develop this "inner knowing?"

_____

_____

_____

_____

WHAT'S THE "NEXT THING" YOU WILL DO?

_____

_____

_____

_____

_____

Tom's Journal: Heart Healing
9. OVERCOMING THE STATUS QUO

This is the major leagues. I've had a few life altering events—graduations, births, marriage, deaths; you know the stuff. But as I follow my cardiologist's guidance to find a surgeon, this is right up there. Met with one today. He seemed fine but something wasn't quite right. He was smart; had some warmth. Some. But a bit impassive for me. Leslie by my side felt similarly. It's clear the surgery will be life changing—transformative. I will be better in many ways—not just the physics of my heart but my spirit may change as well.

Met later in the week with a second surgeon at a different hospital. Dr. N is my guy. Rutgers Med School—I like that, having spent 17 years in the Garden State. Yes, New Jersey is the Garden State. Best tomatoes and sweet corn anywhere. I liked his confidence. Made me feel like this is a piece of cake—that I'll be back 120% in no time. The decision was made. I'm ready to go. Someone said that once you know what it is you need to do (and who's going to help you), fear begins to dissipate. It did.

REFLECTIONS FOR WORK

Facing the work and stress of making a transition is daunting. It's easy to feel so discouraged or overwhelmed that action is impossible. Many internal and external forces are working against you as you begin to collect yourself. When you have a job, boss or a work environment that is debilitating, it's natural to feel a desire to move on. You may even dust off your resume or have someone look at your LinkedIn profile.

But at some point, reality hits—getting something better is going to be difficult. And you may loose heart as well as momentum.

William Willimon, Methodist bishop and theologian says, "The status quo is strongly alluring. It is the air we breathe, the food we eat, the six-thirty news, our institutions, theologies and politics. The only way we shall break its hold on us is to be transferred to another dominion, to be cut loose from our old certainties, to be thrust under the flood and then pulled forth fresh and newborn."

Willimon is preaching about spiritual transformation but it works for career, job and retirement too. We often need a profound event in our lives to get us going. And the resulting pressure can actually help us make a good decision and get you moving toward new, meaningful work. As you take little steps and feel your confidence returning, good things happen. An encouraging word from a colleague or supervisor can help get you unstuck. Sending just one text or email to a potential new contact can provide important energy.

PONDER

What event or experience have you had which might bring a sense of urgency to your life?

_____

_____

_____

_____

What important issues need to be addressed in this stage of your life?

_____

_____

_____

_____

What clarity do you have on your talents and how people and organizations can benefit from them?

_____

_____

_____

_____

Is there someone who can help you get moving toward more satisfying work?

_____

_____

_____

_____

What do you need to do to break the allure of the status quo?

_____

_____

_____

_____

WHAT'S THE "NEXT THING" YOU WILL DO?

_____

_____

_____

_____

Tom's Journal: Heart Healing
10. YOUR FEARS ARE NOT YOU

I wish this surgery wasn't happening but by accepting it, I feel stronger. Ironic—I am strong in my weakness. The disciple Paul said something like that. (2 Corinthians 12:10)

I guess that adds up because when we are afraid and things are out of our control, we have only one place to turn—the Holy Presence in, above and around us. God.

I wrote my obituary today. Seemed like a good thing to do. I don't believe it's going to be printed anytime soon but it allowed me to reflect on what's important in my life and how I want to be remembered. Good stuff for anyone, I believe. It also boosted my morale to examine my accomplishments and priorities. Not a bad thing either in times like this. Any port in a storm.

REFLECTIONS FOR WORK

"Face your fears" is one of those pieces of advice that leaves us wanting. Not specific enough. Sounds good but not really helpful. Writer, educator and "recovering sociologist" (his humor!) and fellow Wisconsinite Parker Palmer helps us.

He says of course we will be afraid of things. It's the human reaction to perceived danger. But we don't have to be our fear, he suggests. What he means by that is that if we examine our fear, we may find something stronger so we aren't paralyzed. As we go into our fear, we often find it's not so bad and we discover ways of addressing it. We have resources. Our faith, people who care about us, and preparation can all make a difference.

Episcopal priest and spiritual writer, Barbara Crafton, talks about how we are able to get through tough times by staring the difficulty down and allowing our soul to be open to its natural, sacred strength. "When did the collision between our appetites and the needs of our souls happen? Was there a heart attack? Did we get laid off from work, one of the thousands certified as extraneous? Did a beloved child become a bored stranger, a marriage fall silent and cold? Or, by some exquisite working of God's grace, did we just find the courage to look the truth in the eye and, for once, not blink?"

As we wonder and worry about the changes surrounding us, let's consider all our resources, especially those we can't see. Believing in the loving, caring people around us and in our own "sacred strength" is a good beginning.

PONDER

How will you strike the balance between examining the fears surrounding this transition and not be immersed in them?

_____

_____

_____

_____

What resources might you uncover and how will they help you? How will you "look the truth in the eye" and see how doable this transition really is?

_____

_____

_____

_____

WHAT'S THE "NEXT THING" YOU WILL DO?

_____

_____

_____

_____

NOTES

Tom's Journal: At the End with Dad
11. TURNING TO GOD

I remember the phone call with my Dad when the wheels started to come off. It began as one of our regular visits with job, kids, Packers and his latest tennis outing the focal points. Good stuff. My Dad had successful bypass surgery a few years back and also had some cancerous moles removed from his chest about that time too. Things had gone well for awhile.

The conversation then turned to health and that he had been to both his cardiologist and oncologist in the past week. A hole formed in my gut. He told me how they had discovered that some cancer now inside his chest was interfering with his pacemaker. And that surgery was going to be required. I did my best to be encouraging, loving—but knew that it was one of those times when words are surely meaningless. I said goodbye with a stomachache and wet eyes. Felt lost. The only place to turn was God. I had no idea how and where.

REFLECTIONS FOR WORK

In the work of making a successful transition, we often find obstacles which drop us in our tracks. Sometimes it's discouragement due to rejection letters, unsuccessful interviews or people turning us down for meetings. Or it's that painful encounter with your boss where it appears your work isn't appreciated. Hope begins to wane. We've been doing all the right stuff, but new, meaningful work seems far out of reach.

In Acts 7, Luke tells how Stephen is preaching to the Pharisees and gets carried away. He criticizes the Jewish leaders with harsh words about being stiff-necked old men, and asking them why they are always resisting the Holy Spirit.

I often direct Stephen's question to myself and find the image compelling. Sometimes I just "know" that I need to turn to God. Do something to bring God into the picture, taking time to follow the Spirit's lead. Maybe it's going to Mass, listening to sacred music, journaling, giving the Eucharist or simply pausing to reflect on the blessings in my life. Something. Anything.

The lesson is clear. Listen and act on the callings from the place where God interacts with our individual souls. Soul is a slippery idea but Parker Palmer in his book, *Hidden Wholeness,* helps us understand it: "Philosophers haggle about what to call the core of our humanity, but I am no stickler for precision. Thomas Merton, prolific writer and social activist monk from the 1950's and 60's, called it the 'true self.'

Buddhists call it original nature or big self. Quakers call it the inner teacher or inner light. Hasidic Jews call it a spark of the divine. Humanists call it identity and integrity. In popular parlance, people often call it soul. That life giving core of living self, with its hunger for truth and justice, love and forgiveness. What we name it matters little. That we name it matters profoundly."

And that we embrace it, wrestle with it and apply it to our transition. We know this work is necessary, right and good—and from God. It's so common to get lost in the jungle of job seeking activities, ignoring our soul. We must not.

PONDER

What's holding you back from bringing a new or renewed Spiritual practice into your transition work in a more intentional, integrative way?

What practices have brought you intimacy with God and hope in your life?

WHAT'S THE "NEXT THING" YOU WILL DO?

_____

_____

_____

_____

_____

Tom's Journal: Heart Healing
12. ACTING ON FEAR

Home early today from the CT Scan to see how large the aortic aneurysm is—this will help determine when to do the surgery. If close to 5 cm, it's game time. If less, wait a year or so. Dr. N calls at 3 and I'm glad my wife Les will be by my side with her usual high octane questions. Someone said something like this once, "Nothing makes your priorities clearer than a death sentence." Less so but still true of facing open heart surgery. My life priorities have been clearer lately. More straightforward. The important things are just that; others not so much. A silver lining. I think that's true for any crisis. Yep. Priority one, get my heart fixed.

REFLECTIONS FOR WORK

More on fear—our main stumbling block in moving on to more satisfying work. Of course we're afraid. We're asking ourselves to move from things we know to that which we don't. Parker Palmer courageously said that he thinks Jesus didn't really mean it when he told his disciples not to be afraid when he walked on the Sea of Galilee. He meant that we need to recognize what it is we are afraid of—and then take steps toward addressing that fear. Parker also emphasized that "we can't be our fear." We need to find other things in our lives which are stronger. Many of us allow fear to paralyze us because we don't like how it feels. But if you allow yourself to feel the fear when it shows up, it often lessens and the challenges appear more manageable.

As we move to positive activity, good things happen. Hope occurs. We see light, and the meaning we long for in new work comes into focus. Activity increases and we are able to observe progress. Networking begins to pay off. Our goals become clearer and we emerge more articulate, persuasive in presenting them to those who can help us. When this happens, employers and those we network with more easily see how we can add value to their organizations. A powerful outcome.

PONDER

How will you move forward when gripped by the fears of transition?

_____

_____

_____

Make a list of ideas. Reflect and pray on them. Bring them to a trusted friend or mentor.

_____

_____

_____

_____

WHAT'S THE "NEXT THING" YOU WILL DO?

_____

_____

_____

_____

NOTES

Tom's Journal: At the End with Dad
13. PREPARING, LISTENING, RESPECTING

I talk to Dad; he's staring out the window so I unwisely ask, "Do you see your brother Bob or sister Gert"? (They had died several years ago.) He gives me "the look"—the one that has sunk me for 56 years when I realized I screwed up. He responds, "Don't do that. It's not helpful."

Good lesson. Let the guy be where he is—not where you want him to be. He's still got enough spirit to shame a son—and teach a lesson. Thanks Dad, I think.

REFLECTIONS FOR WORK

There are many intense interactions throughout the transition process. Interviews are stressful since so much is on the line. Telephone discussions need to be rehearsed as outcomes lead to more advanced meetings. Networking encounters must be both polished and genuine— a challenging proposition for all of us. Maybe most importantly, we need to know our audience—the individual with whom we're speaking and what matters most to him or her. Blathering on about all our accomplishments will not prove effective. Even asking well researched, penetrating questions can get us in trouble if the timing is off or the intent is self-serving.

We must put ourselves in their shoes. What is the central objective for this conversation? What will be most useful or meaningful to the audience? How can I be considerate of them and respectful of their organization? Which of my experiences or accomplishments are best connected to their needs, and how can I introduce them gradually so they will then draw me out with questions?

Developing rapport and mutual respect with the person results in an effective balance between speaking and listening. Once this is established, you will be in a better position to effectively present your work accomplishments. And how specifically you can benefit a potential new employer.

PONDER

How will you prepare for your next meeting or interview?

_____

_____

_____

_____

How will you ensure that you are sensitive to your listener's needs throughout the conversation?

_____

_____

_____

_____

Write down topics and even phrases you want to avoid during the meeting as well as thoughtful approaches if these topics come up.

_____

_____

_____

_____

WHAT'S THE "NEXT THING" YOU WILL DO?

_____

_____

_____

_____

Tom's Journal: Heart Healing
14. MAKING THE RIGHT MOVE

So here I am, alone in the admitting room of Froedtert Hospital and Medical College of Wisconsin. Just finished calls to my wife, brothers Jack, Jim and Bill, Feds, a friend from high school and college, cousin Mary, and my secretary at UW Milwaukee—feeling pretty talked out. We're getting it done on Thursday, two days from now. Following several days of concern about "sensations" in my chest— not pain as I was sure to add whenever telling someone. I went to the Heart and Vascular Center last Friday to have an EKG. Results were fine. Came home but forgot my journal in the waiting room.

Returned on Monday to retrieve it and told Rebecca, the PA, I still had the "sensations." She smiled but escorted me into the exam room— did one more EKG; it's still fine, but she called Dr. N, hangs up and says emphatically, "Dr. N said, "Admit him, cath him; we're doing it tomorrow!" OK—it's on! I'm grateful...and scared. Hopeful and confident. God's in it. I will get a repaired heart; it will tick like a Swiss watch.

No small deal here. Open heart surgery. Five hours. Body temperature lowered while I'm placed on an artificial heart and they cut down the middle through the breastbone; take out the old valve and replace it with a new, porcine (pork and synthetic material). Then repair the aneurysm in the aorta. Piece of cake.

This does feel mixed up. I will be the guy in the movie. With tubes in him. Not the visitor who comforts or who prays with the person in the bed. Catheterization went great. The techs were funny, compassionate and professional. I liked them. The rest of my heart is great. No bypasses needed. Let's go.

REFLECTIONS FOR WORK

It's easy to put off big things like a job change and by rationalizing that things are OK as is. Philosophy like "the devil we know is better than the one we don't" promotes the pessimism which drives immobility. Most of us will admit we have stayed in some jobs too long. What are the clear signals that you need to move on other than the obvious like you hate getting up for work, you dread Mondays, you despise your boss, and your work has not progressed with challenge, depth and variety.

J.T. O'Donnell, career writer, has four more:

- ❖ You only think about your work 9-5, Monday—Friday,
- ❖ You break the 80-20 rule—you should be "happy" with 80% of your total job,
- ❖ You don't read about your field any more—or very little,
- ❖ You look for any excuse for a day off.

Sometimes, someone else needs to get you moving. I still regret giving tenure to a loyal colleague, friend and supervisee. He needed to move on to more challenges. He was better than the job he had done well for eight years. By granting tenure, he languished for the next 10 years. We both agreed (later) that it was a poor decision - but the least painful at the time. It can be hard to cause pain but there are times we simply must. Finding a new more satisfying career direction or opportunity hangs in the balance.

PONDER

What work decisions have you wrestled with for too long?

_____

_____

_____

_____

If you could snap your fingers and be in a new work situation, would you? What would it look like?

_____

_____

_____

_____

Who or what can get you moving?

_____

_____

_____

_____

WHAT'S THE "NEXT THING" YOU WILL DO?

_____

_____

_____

_____

Tom's Journal: A Cancer Journey
15. DOING MORE WITH LESS

I wouldn't be writing or living this if I hadn't been diagnosed with this disease. I wouldn't be who I am this moment if I didn't have it. And who am I this moment? In many ways, I am who I always have been– a dad, husband, son, uncle, counselor, teacher, athlete, leader, and friend; a child of God. All those roles and relationships. They haven't changed.

And yet, with this illness and new perspectives which have come from it, I am also one who is spiritually stronger and sees important matters with more clarity, richness, and understanding. I value the present more. I enjoy simple things in new ways. I appreciate competent, compassionate healthcare professionals like I never did before; I feel a deeper sense of gratefulness for life. And yes, I also am more willing to look at death and be less afraid. In a true sense, I am somehow better. I still have my faults to be sure. Just ask the people who are closest to me. But this very moment, although my bodily health is less—I am more.

John O'Donohue's poem "For Absence" reinforces this idea.

For Absence

May you know that absence is alive with hidden presence,

That nothing is ever lost or forgotten.

May the absences in your life grow full of eternal echo.

May you sense around you the secret Elsewhere

Where the presences that have left you dwell.

May you be generous in your embrace of loss.

May the sore well of grief turn into a seamless flow of presence.

May your compassion reach out to the ones we never hear from.

May you have the courage to speak for the excluded ones.

May you become the gracious and passionate subject of your own life.

May you not disrespect your mystery

through brittle words of false belonging.

May you be embraced by God in whom dawn and twilight are one.

May your longing inhabit its dreams within the Great Belonging.

REFLECTIONS FOR WORK

I may have been one of the first to call Leslie, my spouse of 46 years, "Les." She was raised in a traditional Minnesota family with English roots, and everyone used the more formal "Leslie." But the casualness of "Les" seemed to suit our relationship better. And I decided that if I ever had a sailboat I could cleverly name it "The Les is More." Never happened.

Sometimes less really is more and good can come from loss even in something as significant as career or job matters. Strength, courage and new opportunities we never imagined. Of course, this kind of clarity stays well hidden in the early stage of loss. Disbelief, disappointment, anger, uncertainty, and worry about the future provide effective camouflage.

When Chuck Pagano, head coach of the Indianapolis Colts, was diagnosed with leukemia, his inspirational email to his team and fans had the line, "We all will be better for this," referring to his illness and those who were supporting him. I love the insight there. Hard for people on the sideline to understand but on the field, I get it. The helped and the helpers benefit. I tried to get that perspective in the early stage of my diagnosis.

As we leave jobs we may have had for some time, it can be useful to reflect on what we're leaving behind. If we're honest, there are things we won't miss. More importantly, these losses allow us to be stronger in new, significant parts of our lives.

PONDER

How has your transition made you stronger or braver in facing the future?

_____

_____

_____

_____

How can you use this strength in the work which is required to get that next job?

_____

_____

_____

_____

Make a list of how you or your significant others may be "better," closer, or stronger.

_____

_____

_____

_____

WHAT'S THE "NEXT THING" YOU WILL DO?

_____

_____

_____

CHAPTER TWO

MIDDLES

STAGE

MIDDLES

EMOTIONS

Confusion and uncertainty over the future. Skepticism. Ambivalence over the work required. Frustration over failed strategies. Feeling stuck. Hope begins as some progress can be seen or imagined.

KEY TASKS

Commit to exploration and deep research of organizations/ opportunities. Engage key people in my field for direction, support, ideas, referrals i.e. true networking. Achieve balance between using web and personal resources.

SPIRITUAL QUESTIONS

What will I do to reassure myself that hope is alive; that what I'm doing and how I'm praying will continue to be meaningful?

**IGNATIAN REFLECTIONS **

In my uncertainty, immobility or beginning progress, can I get in touch with my longing for magis (greater good) that God and I desire in my work, communicating how my gifts (concrete self) can contribute to others, organizations and the world?

NOTES

Tom's Journal: A Cancer Journey
1. THANKFUL FOR PIECES OF LIGHT

Sometimes on life travels, it appears like we end up where we started. For me, it was a return to a favorite source of wisdom, "Little Pieces of Light" by Sister Joyce Rupp.

This was a poem I'd shared many years ago with a close friend whose husband was dying, and now it offered me strength. So here I am, back to Sister Joyce–this soulful, eloquent nun who was kind enough to say yes to my request to meet my Mom and Dad for a special couple of hours. They were big fans. She gathered with them for coffee and as I watched from a distance; they chatted like old friends. The three made a magical picture. Grace. Now she dares to help me see the good things which might come out of this trial. Light in the darkness of a cancer diagnosis.

As I ended the diagnosis phase, I knew what I was dealing with and what I had to do to get healthy again. The chemotherapy road was clear. Uncertainty became certain. Six months of treatment with three drugs, one as part of a clinical trial I elected. I was told that the side effects would be minimal and I'd likely keep my hair. Music to my ears. And nourishment for my prayer life, now kicking in at a higher level.

REFLECTIONS FOR WORK

There are many new work challenges in the "Middles" part of the William Bridges model. It's hard to be in the midst of change where strategies and outcomes are unclear. Bridges reassures us that "seeds of hope" are planted in this chaos. The English novelist John Galsworthy was on target when he wrote, "the beginnings (and middles) of all human undertakings are untidy."

Perhaps it's a good time to look backwards for old sources of comfort in this time of uncertainty. Maybe there are lessons to be used again. Old friends and colleagues to contact. New letters and emails to write. Dusting off those creative ideas for work projects and endeavors. Coming up with enhancements for your resume, Facebook page, LinkedIn profile, emails and texts can be inspiring. It's a good time to imagine what that better job will look like. And maybe too there's an opportunity to jump-start your spiritual life.

PONDER

Think back on a trial overcome or a situation managed and name something that helped you through it.

_____

_____

_____

_____

How might this lesson be valuable now as you face new challenges in the work ahead?

_____

_____

_____

_____

What resources can you resurrect for new inspiration?

_____

_____

_____

_____

WHAT'S THE "NEXT THING" YOU WILL DO?

_____

_____

_____

_____

Little Pieces of Light
Darkness & Personal Growth

by Joyce Rupp

PRAYER

O God

As I look back on my life,

I see many little pieces of light.

They have given me hope and comfort

in my bleak and weary times.

I thank you for the radiance

of a dark sky full of stars,

and for the faithful light of dawn

which follows every turn of darkness.

I thank you for loved ones and strangers

whose inner beacons of light

have warmed and welcomed my pain.

I thank you for your Presence in my depths,

protecting, guiding, reassuring, and loving.

I thank you for all those life-surprises

Which sparked a bit of hope in my ashes.

And yes, I thank you for my darkness

(the unwanted companion I shun and avoid)

Because this pushy intruder comes with truth

and reveals my hidden treasures to me.

NOTES

Tom's Journal: A Cancer Journey
2. SEEING THE DEEPER THINGS

I am nervously awaiting another assessment of how I've been doing in my battle. Of course I'm longing for spectacular news but I need to guard against being overly hopeful.

No matter what, my life will continue to grow, possibly even flourish. And from the work that takes place in my soul, I believe God is involved; somehow, somewhere, in some clear but also in unknown, mysterious ways. A part Christian Wiman's poem, "Every Riven Thing" strengthens me.

> *God goes, belonging to every riven thing he's made...*

> *Think of the atoms inside the stone...*

> *think of the man who sits alone...*

> *A part of what man knows...*

> *Apart from what man knows...*

> *God goes belonging to every riven thing he's made.*

Riven—a most interesting word. Torn apart, split, divided. Well, chemotherapy certainly does that. But after being split apart, life grows again. I offer myself to this truth. As I wait for results from my scan following six months of chemotherapy, I try to not get too caught up in what I want from the outcome. Easier said than done.

REFLECTIONS FOR WORK

The work of making a successful transition is characterized by decisions that we control, e.g., How should I change my resume or LinkedIn profile? When and how can I follow-up the successful networking discussion? What's an effective way of repositioning my work with ABC Company to impress the recruiter from DEF, Inc.? How can I get more value with my mentor?

We also have to manage decisions from network contacts, recruiters, and employers over which we have little control. Usually none. Often these decisions aren't in our favor. Employers tell us they've decided to go in another direction, the fit's not quite right, another candidate has more of this or that, business dictates a freeze on hiring…blah blah blah. Although challenging, to say the least, it's important to keep a positive view and look for the silver lining.

Taking a deeper view of things can make a difference in allowing you to put things in perspective and store up necessary strength. While waiting for decisions that you can't control, it's important to reaffirm the good things you did. Take comfort in knowing you performed your best while shaping new strategies for the future. And count the positives gained and lessons learned from the experience.

PONDER

What aspects of your life have been split up or destroyed in
this transition?

_____

_____

_____

How can this be viewed in a potentially positive light?

_____

_____

_____

Did you meet new people who can help? What information
or resources can be used as you continue your transition work?

_____

_____

_____

WHAT'S THE "NEXT THING" YOU WILL DO?

_____

_____

_____

NOTES

Tom's Journal: Mom's Dying

3. WE KNOW MORE THAN WE THINK

Sitting with Mom again. I think about how anxious I was before I walked into the room. Last week, Leslie and I cried when we saw her looking so old and helpless. Before entering the room of a dying mom, it's impossible to know what you're about to see—or what emotions are going to rise.

Now as I sit with my Mom while she sleeps, I feel guilty and not very loving. I'm remembering the times I'd tell people that my Mom was not that smart. I acknowledged that she had good practical sense and could light up a room with her charm and beauty. But I rarely respected her mind.

Then I recall how later in life I heard her say, "I like what I know." The comment caught me by surprise as I reflected on its truth. Our talents are usually the intersection of our interests and our abilities or knowledge. It's what we do best. It's why we get hired to do a specific job. Our passion for work starts with liking what we know. Way to go, Mom.

REFLECTIONS FOR WORK

When I'm speaking or coaching on the art and science of networking, people seem incredulous that a stranger would want to talk to them. The common view of networking is asking a friend what they know about job opportunities. True networking is believing you have something important to say or ask in your field and finding the right opportunity to execute the conversation with the right person. Easier said than done, but it begins with believing in yourself—and doing deep research into the important issues of your work. When you own that new knowledge you'll be confident about sharing it. As Joe Sweeney says in *Networking is a Contact Sport,* "There is only one letter difference between not working and networking."

So, my Mom does have things to teach us. Even now, as I reflect on her gentle wisdom, she also had this wonderful, respectful way of letting you know when she was ready to end a conversation. She would humbly say, "I guess that's all I know." On a deeper level, it also says to me that we each have limits to our knowledge and expertise— and need to know when to just listen. Asking questions should take over for making pronouncements, usually resulting in a more impressed partner in networking, interviewing or conversation.

Jack Falvey, business writer from way back in 1987, created an inspiring metaphor. Successful transitions require us to get out in the rain where it's cold and wet. That's where the lightning is. It's scary but also strikes in the form of inspiration, energy and connections with people we don't know. As new relationships grow, they are often the ones which can make a difference in our journey. Jack still has the best article ever on networking, posted on the Center for Life Transitions' website.

PONDER

Where does interest, ability and knowledge come together for you? How can this be shaped into an observation or question which someone in your field would like to discuss?

How can you get by the self-defeating myth that no one wants to meet with me to discuss important happenings in my field?

What new research might you do to gain important, new knowledge or insights?

Think of a time when you talked too much in a conversation and the result was not what you wanted it to be. How will you change this behavior in the future?

_____

_____

_____

_____

WHAT'S THE "NEXT THING" YOU WILL DO?

_____

_____

_____

_____

Tom's Journal: Heart Healing
4. RESTING BEFORE PROCEEDING

This is an excerpt from a note my oldest daughter, Libby, wrote in my journal from the hospital chapel during the hours following surgery.

In the interfaith chapel, there are a variety of wooden symbols on the walls. One is a yin-yang, and looking at its light and dark equal opposites, I think of you, Dad, awake and asleep. You're asleep again now, in the mysterious darkness they settle you into when they need you to be deeply peaceful while they fix something. They're fixing something now, getting some air out of the area next to your lung so your lung can expand and you can breathe on your own.

As you sleep and get the rest you need, I'm sitting out in the lobby, late afternoon sunlight streaming in and warming my back. We're all waiting for your spirit to join us again, here in the light.

REFLECTIONS FOR WORK

The work of transition gets tiresome and tedious. We often need a break and fresh ways of looking at things. And rest. I appreciate the story in the Old Testament about Elijah fleeing his captors into the desert having to stop and rest.

An angel ministers to him, speaking comforting words about resting because the journey is too hard. He falls asleep and wakes to cool water and fresh cakes. He then continues his journey to Mt. Horeb where he listens to the soft voice of God. Rest can be an important element of transition—and can take many forms. The obvious one is that we need to back off from time to time from the hard work and the pressure of job hunting. Making time to exercise, play, laugh with loved ones, eat well, be entertained. Of course, sleep is necessary for our health. Your body and soul know how to restore themselves, getting you back to work with new energy. Poet, Judy Brown, metaphorically expresses it as the need to rest in the trough of the wave before catching the next crest.

Resting from the stressful aspects of transition research, preparation and rehearsal can also mean developing creative ways of approaching the work. Spend time doing things outside the box of conventional job hunting, e.g. post something creative or amusing on LinkedIn; use Facebook to update friends on your progress; search the web for perfect jobs; decrease time on conventional job boards, knowing they seldom pay off; send an email requesting a 15-minute informational meeting with one of the local leaders in your field or industry.

Sometimes we need a new perspective on what we're doing or not doing. Finding rest or the right helper can give us that.

PONDER

Who could you ask to help you take a fresh look at the process you're in making a work, career, or retirement transition?

_____

_____

_____

_____

Think hard and honestly about the rest, relaxation and rejuvenation you are building into the work you're doing to find new employment.

_____

_____

_____

_____

What out-of-the-box strategy or creative move might jump-start your work search?

_____

_____

_____

_____

WHAT'S THE "NEXT THING" YOU WILL DO?

_____

_____

_____

_____

The Trough

by Judy Brown

There is a trough in waves,

a low spot

where horizon disappears

and only sky

and water

are our company.

And there we lose our way

unless

we rest, knowing the wave will bring us

to its crest again.

There we may drown

if we let fear

hold us in its grip and shake us

side to side,

and leave us flailing, torn, disoriented.

But if we rest there

in the trough,

in silence,

being in the low part of the wave,

keeping our energy and

noticing the shape of things,

the flow,

then time alone

will bring us to another

place

where we can see

horizon, see land again,

regain our sense

of where

we are,

and where we need to swim.

Tom's Journal: A Cancer Journey
5. LIKE A MOON RISING

God is in this. I remember sitting next to my friend Joe at "Sloan Kettering Cancer Center in NYC" when he had a few days to live. He could barely speak. I asked him if there was anything good here. Any light for you, Joe, in this darkness? He responded, "Yes, God is here–and it makes all the difference." Blew me away, Joe's faith. If God was there, then God is with me in the next stage of my life as I battle.

I am at some level inarticulately called to this. Thomas Merton's line about God "obscurely calling him" has meaning for me. I will grow spiritually...find fresh work and ministry...meet new people to help and who will be my helpers.

Mira Kirshenbaum said it well, "When you discover the true meaning of the events in your life, everything changes."

REFLECTIONS FOR WORK

In time we move to the "middle" of a transition in the Bridges model. This is when we are past where we were (e.g. no longer in our previous job) but not engaged in the new work we desire.

For me with lymphoma, the period of my life without this disease was past and I wasn't at the stage yet where the disease would hopefully be in remission. I was at the beginning of a "middle"– about to begin chemotherapy. Middles can be difficult, as there is still plenty of uncertainty and regret. There's also some comfort in knowing that the journey has begun.

Relying on Bridges' "seeds of hope", I was beginning to gain some confidence in the doctors and healthcare pros who were treating me. Critical support from Leslie, our kids and good friends was revving up as well. I knew what I had and there was a plan to fight it. Poet, Ranier Maria Rilke, teaches "Everything that happens keeps on being a beginning...perhaps the time when everything in me is working at God."

In examining the middle aspects of transitions with their ambiguity and incompleteness, maybe you're feeling the beginnings of confidence. There's comfort in knowing that the journey toward something better has begun. You've weathered the storm of leaving that old work, and now a plan is forming to get to where you want to be. And you know that support from people who love you, confidence from colleagues who believe in you and a new faith will sustain you. Faith like David Whyte's slender new moon is forming. And maybe that faith is allowing you to see more clearly what still needs to be accomplished to find that new work on the horizon.

PONDER

Write down how you are gaining faith in yourself, others, and something beyond yourself as you distance yourself from the previous work.

_____

_____

_____

_____

What one "seed of hope" can you identify?

_____

_____

_____

_____

What one thing do you have faith in?

_____

_____

_____

_____

WHAT'S THE "NEXT THING" YOU WILL DO?

_____

_____

_____

_____

Faith

by David Whyte

I want to write about faith,

about the way the moon rises

over cold snow, night after night,

faithful even as it fades from fullness,

slowly becoming that last curving and impossible

sliver of light before the final darkness.

But I have no faith myself

I refuse it even the smallest entry.

Let this then, my small poem,

like a new moon, slender and barely open,

be the first prayer that opens me to faith.

Tom's Journal: A Cancer Journey
6. DIFFERENT PERSPECTIVES MATTER

Sunny, cold day at noon as another crossroads looms. We find out how the good guy drugs have been doing in their battle against the bad guy cells in the past three months. I'm trying not to put too much into this deal. If there's progress, great.

Regardless of what these nasty cells are doing or how many are still hanging around, I will continue to fight; my work and play will not stop. Dr. F is not kicking me out of his office. God is not going anywhere; Les, my kids, and my friends are still by my side; all my fortifications are in place. Hope springs eternal, some wise person said. My life is as full and rich as it's always been. My guide on many things, Thomas Merton, reminds me that "perhaps I am stronger than I think."

I find hope in this new outlook. And hope is what I most need.

REFLECTIONS FOR WORK

Finding hope in despair is not easy; sometimes it's not possible. It takes time, support from others and often a radically different perspective. And we have to be willing to look for it.

The "work of transition" is hard, sometimes causing gloom and despondency. There are always setbacks. Although you only need one "yes" from the right employer, there are many, many "no's" before that comes. Often, finding success requires turning our approach to job hunting upside down to find a new perspective. Sometimes we can find hope in our efforts if we can identify a small success. It might come from:

❖ An encouraging word from a friend or mentor

❖ A productive meeting with someone who identifies an opportunity

❖ A successful interview where even though you didn't get the offer, the employer respected you and your qualifications

❖ A valuable piece of research to use in your next networking contact

❖ A different, more positive way of looking at your challenges

I experienced this change in perspective while waiting for test results at an important juncture in my lymphoma treatment. It occurred to me that no matter what the results were, I was still in the "game" and had a lot going for me.

Parker Palmer speaks openly about his depression and how, in his worst moments, he had this dark image of a fist pounding him into the ground. He was able to change that image through the help of a trusted friend. His friend asked how it would be different if that fist was an open hand holding him and gently lowering him to the ground where he could stand and get his bearings. Parker formed this new image—and moved forward with hope he didn't have before.

In job seeking, it's easy to keep seeing ourselves in old ways—ways which can impede our progress. Doing additional research in identifying fresh job leads, organizations or contacts can bring vigor to our job goals. Confiding in that trusted friend, adviser or mentor can bring new life to the process.

There are no quick solutions in the work of transition, but new perspectives keep us going.

PONDER

How can you picture yourself in this transition in a way that is more positive than the images you may have had?

_____

_____

_____

Who can best help you?

_____

_____

_____

_____

What small victories have you had? Let them form the elements of this new picture.

_____

_____

_____

_____

WHAT'S THE "NEXT THING" YOU WILL DO?

_____

_____

_____

_____

Tom's Journal: At the End with Dad
7. I HAD HOPED IT WOULD BE DIFFERENT

My dad was dying. My brothers and I were taking turns caring for him and for Mom. I had come in from Milwaukee with Les on Sunday for my shift. Dad was very weak, rapid breathing, glassy stare, no recognition. Les went in to see him and he raised his arms to her in greeting— his response deeply touched me. She spent some quiet time with him— held his hand and spoke softly to him. I don't know what about— doesn't matter. She was his first of four beautiful daughters-in-law.

Les left with my brother Jim and his wife Mary. I thought it was going to be a quiet night but throughout the evening, Dad needed a lot of help. I got desperate about 10 PM. I thought about calling my old friend and teammate Chuck to come and help—but called hospice. Ellen came out at 11 and restored my confidence. She was gentle and professional. Amazing how much love she showed Dad in moving him and speaking to him—holy stuff. An angel at work.

I got up at 2:00 AM and Mom was also up—said she hadn't slept since 10. I went in to give Dad more morphine. He was still— no raspy breathing. I went slowly to him intent on his lifeless face. I put my ear to his quiet heart —and his breathless mouth. He was cold. My Dad was not there. I stayed by him for 5 or 10 minutes, cradling his head; hugged him, thanked him and then went to Mom. I felt terrible— if I had gone to him earlier, I would have been with him when he died.

I choked—"Dad's gone, Mom." She wept standing in her walker and we cried together. We went to see him and sat on the bed for 45 minutes or so. She told me a wonderful story about their first date - a walk together on the day after Homecoming. Mom and Dad started with different partners but Mom switched because Dad was taller. She said she knew he was the one that first day.

Ellen called the funeral home. I kissed Dad one more time hard on his cheek. "Thanks, Dad—I'm glad you're home." Chad and George came in dark suits and were very reverent. Ellen left, and Mom and I sat in the chairs in the living room and dozed and talked. Hard to believe Dad was gone. I felt weak, hollow.

I had hoped my final moments with him would be different.

REFLECTIONS FOR WORK

There is much to learn from Luke's (24:13-35) account of Cleopas and another of Jesus' disciples walking away from Jerusalem in fear of persecution because of their association with Jesus. Along the road to Emmaus, they encounter a stranger and walk with him. The stranger asks about the events which occurred in Jerusalem including the crucifixion of this man, Jesus. The disciples are amazed he hadn't heard of what happened and proceed to tell him including this poignant statement, "Jesus was mighty in word and deed…he was handed over to the chief priest and leaders; he was condemned and crucified.

We had hoped that he was the one to redeem Israel."

James Martin, S.J. in *Jesus, A Pilgrimage* teaches us about feeling hopeless. He conveys that the words of the disciples here speak of loss and dejection. There are many times in the work of transition when hopelessness is experienced. We often feel like we just can't go on or get the job done. The work is too hard. The way unclear.

The disciples continued with the stranger who explained to them that they "are slow at heart to believe what the prophets taught them about Jesus' resurrection." When they arrived at the village, they invited him to stay. As they broke bread that evening, they realized he was Jesus. Jesus then disappeared but the disciples had their faith strengthened and they returned to Jerusalem to tell the others what had happened. They had "dusted off their faith" by first inviting Jesus to stay with them and then to share a meal with them.

In my dark moments, I often seek the Eucharist for strength. Sometimes, I drive a short distance to the Sisters of St. Francis Motherhouse to walk the outdoor stations. I've developed a short, made-up prayer for each one which connects the station to how my life might be better, stronger.

When we had hoped to be farther along in our search for new work...when we had hoped to have more people in our network advocate for us...when we had hoped to identify more opportunities to use our gifts...when we had hoped to have a more successful meeting...when we had hoped to have a clearer understanding of how to make life more satisfying and spiritual, maybe there are still possibilities along the road to see Jesus.

And find the strength to continue the journey with renewed hope. Like Cleopas and his friend.

PONDER

Name the part of your transition which you find the most challenging and most in need of hope.

_____

_____

_____

_____

What are the resources and who are the people in your life to help you "see Jesus" and gain strength?

_____

_____

_____

_____

WHAT'S THE "NEXT THING" YOU WILL DO?

_____

_____

_____

_____

NOTES

Tom's Journal: A Cancer Journey
8. DOING IT YOURSELF AND WITH OTHERS

Monday, overlooking the campus in my UW Milwaukee office, continuing to work with the news of my cancer. This a good place—a quiet place. I reflect on the people who are supporting me in this hard time. My family is first and foremost, especially my wife, Les. She's right where I need her to be. Most people don't know how to react. They just want me to be well and not have to think about that word "cancer." Can't blame them. A pal from high school really surprised me when I told him of my situation. His sincere concern was expressed in tears as we hugged. I can't describe how nourished I was by his loving reaction.

I wrote earlier about Chuck Pagano, head coach of the Indianapolis Colts, who inspired his team with the statement, "We will all be better for this." A clear statement that the afflicted one is better for the support of the helpers. And the helpers find new perspectives and are better too.

REFLECTIONS FOR WORK

The work of transition is of course all about us. Thomas Merton said to his Buddhist colleagues when he was visiting Tibet during the Korean War, "From now on, Brother, everybody stands on his own two feet."

Job hunting success does come from our individual efforts. No one is going to give us a new job or a clear sense of direction. Whenever I meet with coaching clients for the first time, I'm struck by the loneliness of transition work. I've preached for years about the value—no, the necessity—of not going it alone. We all need support from others when managing change. Friends, family, mentors, coaches, counselors, advisers—each can help in unique ways.

But as I listen to job-seeking stories of people in transition, they are inevitably characterized by frustrations from time-worn strategies conducted on their own. "I've applied for 15 jobs with no interviews." "I sent my resume to 34 places and no one got back to me." "My recruiter doesn't understand what I really want."

I never hear, "I've been really supported by my colleague who helped me reach out to a fresh contact with a new idea for our industry." Why is that?

Yes, we're on our own but having people around us can make all the difference. I believe people in transition require support from others to be successful. It's that hard line to walk when times are tough. Stand on your own two feet, sure. But having someone to lean on and help you up when you fall can make all the difference. And as Coach Pagano says, everyone is better for it.

PONDER

Name those you depend on for support and guidance in your transition. Make a point to thank them.

_____

_____

_____

_____

Now make a list of three others you need to add to your team. In what ways can they help you?

_____

_____

_____

_____

How will you reach out to them?

_____

_____

_____

_____

WHAT'S THE "NEXT THING" YOU WILL DO?

_____

_____

_____

_____

Tom's Journal: Mom's Dying
9. YOUR BEST CONVERSATION IS
NEEDED: LESSONS FROM HELEN ANN

*I felt lost on what to say to Mom. I could tell she was not inter-
ested in the usual topics—my kids, brother Jim's trip to Texas, the
weather. She was doing the hard work of dying. What did I expect?
We talked about the old neighborhood. She started to sparkle as she
remembered names of families—Bojarskis, Paulsens, Lanzers, Niles.
I mentioned Mrs. Shohable babysitting for us. "She always seemed
so old," I mused. Mom said, "She wasn't as old as she appeared." She
said it with confidence and wisdom. I was floored and asked, "What
do you mean, Mom?" "Oh, Mrs. Shohable was smart - she knew
what was going on."*

*We talked about her cousin Jeannie and husband Ron with
whom I never had much contact. I said what I remember about
Jeannie was that she was pretty. Mom asked incredulously, "That's
all you remember about her?" I felt badly for not remembering other,
more important qualities of her cousin. Here was my Mom on
her deathbed, challenging me to know the important things about
people in my life. As Dad would say, "How to go, H.A.!"*

REFLECTIONS FOR WORK

Successful interviewing is hard. Some people say it's all about chemistry. I counter with another view. It's all about preparation. Sure, connecting to the other person in networking and interviewing is critical, but what you say and how you say it can lead to that "chemical reaction." For example:

Employer Question
"How do you feel about calling people and presenting ideas over the phone?"

Little Chemistry
"I don't mind it. I'm a people person and like talking to others."

More Chemistry
"That kind of work invigorates me. I think it's important to know what you want to say in advance—then you can focus on the energy you need for the call. That can get the listener excited about the conversation." Often, it can be important to go deeper in your conversation. Staying on the surface is both safe and easy. It may even feel effective. But going deeper with both content and affect can set you apart from run-of-the-mill candidates.

Employer Question
"Tell me about a situation where you wished you could have managed it differently with better outcomes."

OK Reply
"When I lead groups, I usually pull ideas from the strongest members. As I think back on my latest meeting with ABC Group, I would have liked to have done a better job of getting the whole group involved."

Better, Deeper Reply

"As project head, my boss asked me to move up the deadline for the report. I told my group, and we all agreed that if we did, several other projects would suffer. They asked me to tell my boss, which I did. She was understanding, and everything worked out. In hindsight, I know my boss was disappointed and has kept me from some work which would have advanced my career. If I could do it over, I would have been a tougher manager and figured out ways to meet the tighter schedule."

PONDER

Describe a work experience where you would have done things differently in retrospect. Describe in detail using names, numbers, outcomes and your emotions.

_____

_____

_____

_____

Edit the experience to three to four sentences which demonstrates understanding and professional growth. Have someone review them to ensure they aren't too personal or would make a person in a professional meeting uncomfortable.

_____

_____

_____

_____

WHAT'S THE "NEXT THING" YOU WILL DO?

_____

_____

_____

_____

Tom's Journal: A Cancer Journey
10. GIFTS ARE TO BE DISCOVERED

Gifts from others have been vividly evident to me to as I continue treatment at Froedtert Clinical Cancer Center for my lymphoma. My strength throughout this journey is clearly founded in the combination of compassion and professionalism of the people there. From my oncologist Dr. F., his P.A. Julie, nurses and including the receptionist Kristin, who always remembers my name as we kid about the candy bowl not having my favorites. Their talents are apparent in everything they do.

When I see people using their talents to make a difference in an organization, the work is authentic. This enriches everyone. I see that process in the people who make my experience at the Cancer Center rewarding, even at times joyful!

REFLECTIONS FOR WORK

In over forty years of career transition work, I've spoken the words "self-assessment" hundreds of times. It's an important first phase in working through a job or career transition. Clarifying your goals based on substantive knowledge about personal qualities like interests, skills, values, and talents is an essential accomplishment.

Perhaps the most poignant perspective on self-assessment is gained through describing your gifts. I like the Merriam-Webster Dictionary definition of gift: "faculty, aptitude, bent, talent, genius, a special ability for doing something; often implies special favor by God or nature."

Arthur Miller, author of *Why You Can't Be Anything You Want To Be*, talks about it this way:

"Giftedness is the only means I know of for the ordinary person to make sense out of life. Each one is given a purpose and the drive and competitiveness to achieve that purpose. Meaning is thereby built into the adventure of living for everyone."

Our giftedness is the place where everything important intersects– our interests, skills, values, motivations, and strengths. It doesn't really matter what we call these qualities. When they are in action, they enable us to accomplish meaningful work in ways which matter, contributing mightily to organizations. Not to mention your own well being!

Understanding and communicating your gifts is a cornerstone of successful transitions. But when unclear about work direction, I've found that the fog lifts most often when you are out there in your marketplace interacting with people, Herminia Ibarra,

Professor of 121 *TRANSPIRATIONS* Organizational Management at INSEAD (European Institute of Business Administration) offers central wisdom here.

"We learn who we have been and who we might become— in practice, not in theory–by testing fantasy and reality, through exploration and examination, not just by looking inside. Knowing oneself is critical, but it is usually the outcome of–and not a first input to–the reinvention process. Intense introspection poses the danger that a potential career planner will get stuck in the realm of daydreams."

This is a core teaching; I can't think of anything more important. Boosted confidence, clearer goals and new contacts result.

PONDER

Reflect on the positive impact you have on people, programs and/or processes. How much of this impact is due to a combination of what you do well and that which brings you enjoyment?

_____

_____

_____

_____

Where do your interests, skills and values intersect? Label these gifts. Think hard on how they can be put to use in the work you're doing or want to do.

_____

_____

_____

_____

How can you gain the courage and commitment to Dr. Ibarra's central teaching: experiment, experience and explore opportunities in your field?

_____

_____

_____

_____

WHAT'S THE "NEXT THING" YOU WILL DO?

_____

_____

_____

_____

Tom's Journal: A Cancer Journey
11. THERE'S HOPE IN PREPARATION

Today as I face another treatment, I go deeper inside myself for courage. And as my soul takes me to that place, don't you know an attentive, mysterious God waits with reassuring love. I can do this.

If I turn out whole and healthy through this cancer treatment—perhaps a new faith was involved. If it's not successful, then I still have known God's loves me for 65 years in amazing ways—and I will see God's love in new and undiscovered ways in the years I continue to live.

I lean into Thomas Merton's message that it is every human being's birthright to find themselves at home with God. "I don't need to find my way through the jungle of language and problems that today surround God because whether I understand it or not, God loves me." As Merton says, "God is present in me, lives in me, dwells in me, calls me, saves me, and offers me an understanding and light which are like nothing I ever found in books or heard in sermons."

REFLECTIONS FOR WORK

As I started chemotherapy to counter this lymphoma, I was already feeling more confident. Walking toward my first treatment with Dr. F and Leslie at my sides, tears formed as I felt their support. Love. I recalled Henri Nouwen's line how when you feel disempowered, taking in love can strengthen. Middles are difficult as there is still plenty of uncertainty and regret. There's also comfort in knowing that the journey is under way.

My business colleague Darrell used to say with a wink and a theatrical twang as we finished up a productive meeting, "Bach, we ain't where we wanna be, but at least we ain't where we was." There was always a chuckle and more importantly, hope in that folksy insight.

For me, that was true as I was beginning to gain some confidence in the doctors and healthcare professionals who were treating me, and the critical support from Leslie, our kids and good friends was accelerating. I knew what I had and there was a plan to fight it. All my fortifications were kicking into a higher gear. As you may be experiencing discouragement in this middle part of your transition, it's critical to remind yourself of the resources you have in place. The people who care and want to help you succeed. Be sure you're keeping close to your contacts in the field and marketplace, even when times are tough. They aren't giving up on you.

PONDER

Reflect on how far you've come on this journey, focusing on accomplishments and knowing that the resources that brought you this far will continue.

_____

_____

_____

_____

Compile some evidence that God is alive in this transition and you are finding comfort and confidence as you move ahead.

_____

_____

_____

_____

WHAT'S THE "NEXT THING" YOU WILL DO?

_____

_____

_____

_____

NOTES

Tom's Journal: A Cancer Journey
12. FINDING THE SILVER LINING

I'm not saying having cancer doesn't suck, but in the universe of sucking and suffering, pain and worry which people have and had from the dawn of time, this situation is a drop in the bucket. I've been told my cancer is one of the "better ones."

This isn't about comparing my woes to other people. Everyone's suffering is unique and relative, deserving compassion. But it is about recognizing that our burdens do come with graces.

This Milwaukee area insurance company advertises with a focus on "silver linings." I don't like the concept for selling insurance but I do appreciate its truth in life. There will be good things that come from this cancer journey. People will love me in new ways. I may find new perspectives on my faith which will impact me and maybe others in useful ways. Amen to that.

REFLECTIONS FOR WORK

Ignatius of Loyola said, "In calling me to live my special qualities and characteristics, God planted deep in myself an original purpose—what my concrete self adds up to—and calls me to live that out." As we examine the middle aspects of transition, you can feel good that you are in the center of the Ignatian process. You are working hard to identify and communicate "your special qualities." Living that out is exactly what you're doing as you take steps toward better work.

And you know that support from people who love you, confidence from colleagues who believe in you and a new faith which is forming all will sustain you. Your ideas for new work and how you'll get there are taking shape. The "purpose planted in you" and what your "concrete self" adds up to are becoming a little clearer.

The "heavy lifting" is ahead. But for now

- ❖ You can make a new list of networking contacts,

- ❖ Prepare some powerful language to present your strengths and how they can make a difference for select organizations you're targeting,

- ❖ Refine your research on potential employers focusing on the fit between your experience and their needs,

- ❖ Schedule a meeting with your mentor, advisor or "best colleague" who will support you in this transition,

- ❖ Decide which search engines are best for your field and whether a recruiter will be helpful.

PONDER

How are you finding faith in yourself, others, and perhaps something beyond yourself as you gain distance from the previous work?

_____

_____

_____

_____

What one "silver lining " can you identify in your trials of transition and how might they positively impact you? Others?

_____

_____

_____

_____

WHAT'S THE "NEXT THING" YOU WILL DO?

_____

_____

_____

_____

NOTES

Tom's Journal: Heart Healing
13. GETTING ON WITH IT INSPIRES

5:00 AM ......"We go" as Jeff, my quarterback from Ripon College, would say as our offense took the field. I'm calm; at peace. Les and daughter Libby slept in my hospital room. Lib read the 91st Psalm to me. Dr. N came by to give me confidence. I joked about how I expected him to stay up all night making the best valve in the world.

Up and out the door. I speak with the anesthesiologist. He's relaxed—just the way I needed him. Wife of 39 years is by my side as I remove my crucifix, wedding band and Grandfather's onyx ring. Les and I kiss—I'm off. I look back and wave. She smiles, looking confident. I arrive in the surgery room—everyone greets me and makes me feel like they have it covered. Cool. I drift off happily after several IV's are inserted and the right volume of gas enters my system.

Seven hours later I wake up—it felt like minutes. Breathing tube in my mouth and many hoses coming and going from various body parts. Les, Lib and brother Jim are by my side. Later, Lib tells me she was in tears as I was wheeled in and a doc said to her that he hopes those are tears of joy as her Dad did great.

I'm wheeled back into surgery as some tube needs to be reconnected— small bump in the road. I'm back and I motion brother Jim to come close. I trace "I love you" on his hand and the hands of Lib and Les. Deep gratefulness pulsates through me.

I spend the night in the ICU and dream that I haven't had the surgery yet.

REFLECTIONS FOR WORK

It never ceases to amaze me how many good things need to come together to prepare us for a trial. Some we do ourselves and others just happen—so it seems. When facing work changes, it's easy to get overwhelmed. So much to do—so many unknowns. Negative thoughts abound. The Scottish WWI chaplain Oswald Chambers preaches that when we are confused and confounded, it's because we only have partial visions from God. We can't see the possibilities. He says we need to step back, reflect, pray and then do "the next thing." We'll know what the next thing is. Good stuff - successful transitions consist of a series of "next things."

I tell my clients ad nausea that I can only help them if they are willing to do "the work" of transition. Many don't want to hear it; they often nod assent with little commitment to the process. Resume, e-mails, letters and profiles need to be cogent yet persuasive, customized to job requirements and organizational cultures. LinkedIn must be used efficiently as a tool to spread your gospel and secure face-to-face encounters with key people.

Courage has to be mustered to approach people in your field you don't know but who are in positions to make a difference for you. Preparations for meetings and interviews must be meticulous and thorough. You don't want to speak to a topic cold and risk saying too much or too little. Each response should have 1-2 central points which have been prepared. Speaking them should take about a minute or two at the most. You can say more if asked.

Good things you never anticipated happen for you as well. People you barely know recommend and refer you to others who can help. People who love you prove it by doing far more than expected. And you find those Godly moments of anticipation, excitement, and confidence that you can do this.

New, meaningful employment is on the horizon. Something or Someone bigger than yourself is at work here too. So much to do, and be grateful for too.

PONDER

What's your most important accomplishment so far in this transition? How can you use it to gain confidence in taking a step toward new work?

_____

_____

_____

_____

How can "Something or Someone bigger than yourself" come into this process? How will that help you?

_____

_____

_____

_____

WHAT'S THE "NEXT THING" YOU WILL DO?

_____

_____

_____

_____

Tom's Journal: A Cancer Journey
14. LIGHT IN DARKNESS

I'm in that dark place again. I try to be upbeat about all the grace I see and receive as I proceed through this cancer treatment program. How people support me, love me. The competencies and smarts of the caregivers. Their compassion. All good. Beautiful. But I still have these moments of sadness and deep fear. Confusion and the wish that this never happened.

In the midst of fighting and facing this disease, maybe the challenge is to learn that my life is still rich and good and promising. That I am blessed with people and possibilities in the face of danger and uncertainty. That hope is always alive. That death is certain some time, every time and for everybody; and preparation is important. That God is real in unknown, misunderstood, mysterious but also clear and personal ways. That I have a mission and a ministry here. And my heart will always hunt for what I need and rest in what I already have.

This summary soothes me and helps bring that glimmer of light I so need; that everybody needs when facing tough times. If it would only last.

REFLECTIONS FOR WORK

There are many times in transition where discouragement and doom creep into our psyche. Disappointment is around every corner as our requests for informational meetings are denied, resumes aren't read, and networking connections fail. We're bewildered over how and where to volunteer so we can make a difference while enjoying retirement. As a mentor advised, you will hear way more "no's" than "yes's" in this job-seeking process. We must not take this personally. There are many factors which determine progress and ultimately success; we control only some of them.

Sometimes we encounter situations which test us at deep levels and when examined, teach important lessons. Often there is good that comes out of the bad. "Paradoxically, I have found peace because I have always been dissatisfied. My moments of depression and despair turn out to be renewals, new beginnings." Thomas Merton, yet again.

The marketplace is always tough. But maybe there are good things that come from the challenges or even the discouragements. Hopefully you are getting stronger in your ability to face adversity. Possibly, failures cause us to take stock of ourselves and our strategies. Maybe it's time for a new approach. A new direction. A fresh perspective into what's really important. Getting help from new or different resources may be in order.

Mary Isbister, CEO of the Milwaukee company, Gen Met Corp., encourages us, "In these hard times, I'm one of those eternal optimists. This challenging economy is giving all of us time to step back and say–OK, these opportunities that we've thought about and aspire to--what is it going to take?"

There are opportunities which would not be there if it weren't for the adversity and even suffering we encounter. Spiritual writer and BBC broadcaster Michael Ford writes that "every evil conceals a pure blessing, which we in our blindness would have rebuffed had it been offered to us without painful disguise."

PONDER

What trials are you facing and, specifically, where has the journey been the toughest?

_____

_____

_____

_____

How might these difficulties be shaping how you do the work necessary to be successful in your transition?

_____

_____

_____

_____

What's it going to take for you to find the spirit and resources to be successful in this transition.

_____

_____

_____

_____

How can you forge a new philosophy or insight that will strengthen you?

_____

_____

_____

_____

WHAT'S THE "NEXT THING" YOU WILL DO?

_____

_____

_____

_____

Tom's Journal: Mom's Dying
15. WORDS CAN BE OVERRATED

I sit with Mom. She's dozing or as Dad always said when we caught him napping, "just resting my eyes." As I sometimes do, I balance watching Mom with texting my youngest brother Bill to tell him I'm with her. Bill texts me back requesting I give her a smooch for him. I do and I say it's from her baby boy. She smiles. "You know who your baby boy is, right"? I ask.

She looks puzzled, wrinkles her nose the way we all love. I name her boys. "Tom? Jack? Jim? When I say Bill, she smiles and nods. I ask her to please smile again. She does. "You smile like an angel," I tell her.

She is absolutely beautiful.

REFLECTIONS FOR WORK

One of my favorite axioms is, "Networking is simply saying the right thing or asking the right question to the right person at the right time." This requires thought and preparation—and it's worth the effort. Good impressions are established and relationships move forward. Referrals result. Abstract conversations turn to discussions about concrete opportunities. That's the way it works.

Sometimes, however, what you don't say is just as important. Hold back on sharing your true feelings about your previous job or employer. No one wants to hear complaints or observe your finger pointing. Taking the high road is always best, e.g., "My ideas were not right for the department given other priorities. It was a good decision for both parties to move on."

Body language is important. Our gestures, posture and facial expressions can make all the difference. Smiles disarm and make others comfortable. Standing and walking tall speaks volumes about confidence. Eye contact is essential to connecting conversations. And pausing and smiling as you make your important points is critical to a successful interview.

For example as a reply to an interview question: "As we developed the central points for our case, it became clear that we were missing critical inputs from management. (PAUSE, SMILE) The team then developed a survey which resulted in new data from the executives and a more thorough report. (PAUSE) After the presentation, we received a personal note from the CEO congratulating us on our research." (SMALL SMILE)

PONDER

Reflect on your body language, i.e., posture, facial expressions, eye contact and smile when speaking with others in work-related situations. Ask for feedback from a close colleague on this topic.

_____

_____

_____

_____

Recall a situation when you may have said too much in an interview or meeting. How might it help to prepare for your next discussion to write down points you want to make as well as those issues you may need to diplomatically manage during difficult questions?

_____

_____

_____

_____

WHAT'S THE "NEXT THING" YOU WILL DO?

_____

_____

_____

NOTES

Tom's Journal: The Miracle of Oona

16. FINDING GOD IN THE FOXHOLE

My spiritual director encourages me to ponder how my new granddaughter Oona Mae can be a portal to a more meaningful relationship with God—hmmm. Jesus grew up in Nazareth where there were undoubtedly many babies. There are countless paintings of Jesus tenderly holding small children. They weren't portraits but they are poignant images nonetheless. Jesus said that God's truth is revealed to innocents or children (Matthew 11:25-27). And also that we must be childlike in our hearts (Matthew 18:2-4).

Let's proceed...Oona came from the love of my daughter, Libby, and Oona's father, Seth. And from God's creative love. When I am with baby Oona, I am happy; no, joyful. Like nothing else. I am absorbed in her beauty, originality, purity and innocence. Her holiness permeates the space she is in. I know God in fresh ways because of her. There is no one in my life like Oona Mae.

In the single moment of her birth, she became the center of our family's universe. There is nothing we would not do for her, including sacrifice our lives. A solemn statement.

*Oona is love. Of course we're back to love as we are in all import-
ant matters. This precious, tiny creature gives us hope. Oona Mae—my
portal to love and to my relationship with God. I cannot overplay this
wonder of new life as she stirs the souls of everyone in her presence.*

REFLECTIONS FOR WORK

It is not difficult to lose sight of the important things in life
when involved in a work transition. Weighty matters are at stake.
Providing for family. Using our God-given talents. Contributing
to worthy organizations. Gaining earnings to provide for our children's future. Building a meaningful retirement. All important.

But discouragement and disappointment often characterize
transitions. It's hard work putting yourself out there every day - researching, selling, pitching, scheming, following up. Easy to lose
heart. We all need a way we can count on to find our strength, per-
severance and courage, some type of connection to God. A portal.

Jack Falvey, the sage business writer, said that religion at anytime or anyplace can be helpful. He calls it "foxhole religion." Any
port in a storm is another way of putting it. Trying something out
of desperation may wind up revitalizing.

"Religio" in Latin means to bond with God. Maybe, especially
in times of transition, we have to figure out some way to get any
religion we have into play. I love Richard Bolles' quote, "If we have
an old faith hanging in our closet, it's probably a good time to get
it out and dust it off."

We need to find that portal where God can shine through, even as a glimmer—and provide us the perspective we need in our work lives. And the courage to continue reaching for more satisfying work.

PONDER

Where have you found either comfort or courage in challenging situations?

_____

_____

_____

_____

What are the resources? Who are the people? Where are the places that best connect you to God?

_____

_____

_____

_____

What are your portals to a clearer, deeper understanding of
your life ? How and when will you use them?

_____

_____

_____

_____

WHAT'S THE "NEXT THING" YOU WILL DO?

_____

_____

_____

_____

CHAPTER THREE

BEGINNINGS

STAGE
BEGINNINGS

EMOTIONS
Excitement. Anticipation. Relief. Gratitude. Feeling confident in applying lessons learned to new tasks and work environment.

KEY TASKS
Demonstrate gratefulness to people who help me. Advance in my work and workplace with confidence, caution and preparation for the next transition. Continue to meet with people in my field.

SPIRITUAL QUESTIONS
How do I best acknowledge, respect and celebrate my "reinvented self" in this new work, while continuing preparations and prayers for transitions ahead?

IGNATIAN REFLECTIONS **
In getting close to or actually living my new work, can my heart and dispositions be open to generosity, trust and hope, so my faith can grow in love?

NOTES

Tom's Journal: Mom's Dying
1. HONESTY IS THE BEST POLICY

I'm discouraged today as Mom is not responding to any of my conversational schemes. It's clear she is working hard at making the transition from this world. I can hardly blame her for being unresponsive to my lame attempts to engage her in conversation about the weather, grandchildren or my work. She's tired and weak; her face looks beaten up and her beautiful blue eyes don't shine.

I decide to take a chance. I put my face up to hers and said in a mischievous way, "Mom, Mom...now might be a really good time to tell me that of your four sons, I was always your favorite."

I wait, with a little unease that the question may have been inappropriate. Then she beams a smile—wide and long and begins to shake her head back and forth. Her answer is clear without saying a word. She has me chuckling. She was honest, eloquent and entertaining in giving me the bad news.

REFLECTIONS FOR WORK

It's difficult to walk the line between masterful self-marketing and truthful advertising as we offer our stories to employers on paper, web and in person. Of course we want to present our best selves—and sometimes this entails "stretching" the truth or embellishing an accomplishment. I advise clients that the key question in these dilemmas is, "How comfortable am I in responding to deeper questions which may arise about the story, incident or accomplishment, and how specific and clear are the examples or evidence I can provide to back up my claims?"

Statements of accomplishment without evidence come across hollow, inadequate. Evidence translates to numbers, proper nouns and measurable outcomes and are required in our self-marketing.

Parker Palmer says we need to honor our limitations and sometimes this means we have to admit that we hadn't done the work, achieved the outcome or secured the deal.

"No, Ms. Spencer, I've never had responsibilities with that technology applied to a logistics problem of that nature. I am confident with ABC tools, however, and have successfully used them to meet several procurement challenges. I believe there are valuable connections between the two technologies."

PONDER

Study the description of the position you're interviewing
for and write down your weaknesses. Come up with "bullet
points" for how you want to respond to these issues and how
complementary strengths can still make a positive impression.
Make sure you have evidence for each response.

_____

_____

_____

_____

Review your resume and LinkedIn profile for any
embellishments. Are you confident responding to questions
about them?

_____

_____

_____

_____

Reflect back on times you might have been more honest and open when responding to difficult questions. How can you use this intelligence next time you face similar situations?

_____

_____

_____

_____

Think about saying something to an employer which is a little "out of the box" or surprising but which might elicit a positive response. Check it out with a trusted colleague before trying it.

_____

_____

_____

_____

WHAT'S THE "NEXT THING" YOU WILL DO?

_____

_____

_____

_____

Tom's Journal: A Cancer Journey
2. MANAGING EXPECTATIONS

This is the day I've waited for since beginning chemotherapy six months ago. No balloons or Champagne corks flew, however, as Dr. F stated matter-of-factly, "Well, scans are good, you're in full remission." This was the goal from day one so I should be jumping up and down. Not sure what I was hoping for. I guess, "You now have perfect health and you'll live as long as you want, never worrying about anything again!"

Back to earth. I continue with a maintenance plan designed to forestall the cancer's return. There's uncertainty and work ahead. But as I gather myself over this page, I am happy. I am relieved. I am strong.

And yes, I have found meaning and focus from this experience— and will continue to.

REFLECTIONS FOR WORK

The iconic football coach Vince Lombardi said we achieve excellence by chasing perfection. Definitely, but we also mess up by getting expectations out of line with what's realistic or possible. I recount meetings where I thought everything went perfectly. I had done all that I could to present the full value of my project, program or myself. Leaving the room, I reveled in the smiles and acclamations. It wasn't until later that reality hit. Issues I hadn't thought of, planned for or in cases couldn't control drove a decision to go forward without my services.

Walking that line between expecting the best while preparing for the worst is not easy. I was surprised at how much I had to readjust my expectations even after I received the good news that my lymphoma was in remission.

Thomas Merton chimes in as usual. Although he believed his vocation was to head a new monastery in Central America, his superiors in Rome saw otherwise. He eventually realized his true calling— to stay and continue at Gethsemane, his home monastery in Kentucky. But he wasn't happy about it. His biographers, Patrick Hart and Jonathan Montaldo said it well in their introduction to *The Intimate Merton*. "He surrendered himself to the slow heart work of seeking his faith one day at a time and one night at a time in the place where his eyes opened and shut. He got up and fell down, he got up and fell down, and he got up over and over again."

That description is for all of us. We keep falling and getting up, over and over. It's the challenge of life. It's job seeking and career transitions at their core. Having loved ones to share it with and a faith where some strength and guidance can be found make all the difference.

PONDER

How are you managing your expectations for success in
your transition work?

_____

_____

_____

_____

Reflect on the lessons learned from both the successes and
failures in your transition and/or job seeking.

_____

_____

_____

_____

What will you keep doing the same because you know in
your heart it's effective and consistent with who you are?
What will you change?

_____

_____

_____

_____

WHAT'S THE "NEXT THING" YOU WILL DO?

_____

_____

_____

_____

Tom's Journal: Heart Healing
3. FINDING OUR SPIRIT

An excerpt from a note my daughter, Libby, wrote in my journal from the hospital chapel during the hours following my surgery.

In this time before, during, and after your surgery, I've been feeling your spirit so strongly, in a way that I never had before. In your absence, sometimes, I will suddenly get this sense of you, and it's so clear: who you are, the essence of you, your fire. Sometimes, I feel a trace of it in the small things I see around the house, objects that remind me of you and of our interactions.

When they let us visit you just now, you had been awake for a bit, your spirit expressing itself again, whispering softly, out here in the world of light. Your eyes were open, and we were standing around talking to you and holding your hands. You were tied down against the natural impulse to get all those crazy tubes out of your mouth. But you kept gesturing in these familiar ways, gently shrugging and turning your hands up as if to say, "I don't know, it's out of my hands. I'm just along for the ride."

That was your spirit, in those gestures: your strength and humor, your determination to accept what is. I think you know very clearly that the best path is to be open to what's happening, even if it's this hard. Mouth and throat full of plastic, breathing with a machine, IVs everywhere, drugs coursing through your veins, hands tied down. You shrug, good-naturedly.

REFLECTIONS FOR WORK

The mystery and truth of "spirit" is pretty elusive. We know we are more than body and mind—there are too many mysteries inside and outside for that not to be. Deep thinkers like Teilhard de Chardin, Jesuit paleontologist, says we are spiritual beings first who inhabit a human body temporarily, not merely humans who have a spiritual life.

So, great…what does this mean for us as we face life challenges? For conventional Christians, Muslims, Jews, Hindus, Buddhists etc., it translates to prayer. Prayer is communication—sometimes using words—written, spoken, or pure thoughts. Prayer can simply be feelings we have. Or sometimes nothing we do at all as the apostle Paul teaches that the Spirit prays for us in our weakness (Romans 8: 26-27). If we are spiritual, then it means there is something beyond us to which our spirit connects. Divine, Higher Power, Presence, Holy, God, call it what you will. Prayer is a means to communicate or commune. Strength, peace and guidance may come from that. Even specific outcomes, if that is our belief.

I don't know why I don't start every day with a visit to the Irish Jesuits website, Sacred Space. Each time I do, I connect to something good, an inner feeling of love, peace, courage, well-being, gratefulness. It varies. The site consists of a series of short writings on sequential screens following the Ignatian model for prayer.

Perhaps the best way of describing my experience there is Presence. When Moses asked Yahweh his name, Yahweh replied "I am who I am," meaning "I am present." It's this reassuring Presence I find at Sacred Space, facing challenges each day, and throughout my life transitions.

In feeling lost or lethargic in the work of transition, maybe it's this Presence that is most critical to regaining direction. Those indescribable but yet real feelings of strength or possibilities or hope can make all the difference. Prayer and Presence can move us to stay the course on important tasks like writing a revised version of our goal statement, securing another recommendation for our portfolio, developing a fourth question to ask in a meeting, conducting one more web search for information on a potential employer or polishing our elevator speech. These empowered accomplishments can be just what we need to know in our soul that success is in sight.

PONDER

How do you respond to University of Notre Dame theologian Richard McBrien's definition of spirituality? "It's simply living your life knowing there is more to it than meets the eye."

_____

_____

_____

_____

What aspects of your transition require more help than the preparation you do yourself—and the assistance you receive from other people?

_____

_____

_____

_____

How can prayer and Presence help you throughout this transition?

_____

_____

_____

_____

WHAT'S THE "NEXT THING" YOU WILL DO?

_____

_____

_____

_____

Tom's Journal: Heart Healing
4. GOING DEEPER AS WE BEGIN ANEW

It's the second day of recovery and my daughter Emmy from Minneapolis is here! Great to laugh with her as she asks how my "ticker thing" is working out. I see my old pal Feds in the back of the room and motion him over. I tell him "thanks" as I hear he's been hanging around the previous three days! He laughs as I kiddingly say that I saw him scrubbing in with Dr. N. Feels good to joke. Son Jay calls and we talk in heartfelt ways. My cousin Mary and husband Jim bring me some beer, for which I'm not quite ready. Gratefulness permeates my being.

What am I learning? God is in this place. And in the confidence I felt throughout everything. Dr. N, his team, the nurses, family, friends. Such professionalism. Compassion. Love. Wife Leslie by my side, staying close throughout it all.

Where am I going? What have I learned? Many places….and much. All part of the journey. This great, crazy, mysterious journey.

Amen

REFLECTIONS FOR WORK

One of the wisdoms at any juncture of transition but maybe most importantly, during the beginning stage of something new, is to have an appreciation for what we have and have had our whole life long. Family, friends, faith, work.

Christopher Lowney, former Jesuit seminarian, Wall Street executive and author of *Heroic Leadership* and *Pope Francis: Why He Leads the Way He Does*, talks about the importance of wisdom in our decision-making in Proverbs 3:13-15: "Blessed are those who find wisdom, those who gain understanding, for she is more profitable than silver and yields better returns than gold." Most of us spend our lives pursuing "silver." Or a paycheck and what a paycheck buys. And careers which we thought would satisfy. Wisdom is one of those old school words. Its root means "seeing" or "knowing" and implies that we need to examine longer term, more meaningful outcomes from the decisions we make and the directions we pursue.

I think wisdom also infers that we look at deeper questions as we consider new paths. Questions of vocation, that unique "call" from our true heart or soul, not just an analysis of our skills or abilities or even values. Several profound thinkers give us examples:

- ❖ "Who are we and Whose are we?" (Dietrich Bonhoeffer),
- ❖ "Is what I am living, my true life?" (Parker Palmer),
- ❖ "Where do the world's deepest hungers and my best gifts intersect?" (Frederick Buechner),
- ❖ "What am I longing for in my life—in my work?" (Ignatius of Loyola),
- ❖ How do I better understand my soul and its relationship to my life? (Mary Oliver).

Vocation is a slippery idea. It's a call toward something new from something/someone beyond ourselves—while often taking us to places we already know. It is using the gifts we've always had but may need to be rediscovered. Ignatius of Loyola, founder of the Jesuits, provides the best explanation as presented by Jim Manney in his book *God Finds Us:*

"Beneath the love of money, possessions, honor, and pride, we will find what we really want. And here is Ignatius's great insight. When we find what we really want, we find what God wants, too. It's a pretty remarkable idea, so I'll say it again: when we discover what we really want, we discover what God wants, too."

PONDER

What wisdom about your present life do you already have?

_____

_____

_____

_____

What deeper questions might you ponder and how will it relate to your search for better, more meaningful work?

_____

_____

_____

How do you feel about your talents and the world's needs coming together?

_____

_____

_____

Engage the exercise on "Soul" using Mary Oliver's poem in the Appendices.

_____

_____

_____

WHAT'S THE "NEXT THING" YOU WILL DO?

_____

_____

_____

Tom's Journal: Heart Healing
5. TAKING IN LOVE

I'm home! Amazing that it's been only four days since my surgery. Recovery went smoothly. I was up walking in no time and although the nine-inch cut into my torso is serious—-pain is little and it will heal nicely. Rehab will be a challenge and I'm sure I'll wonder for a while how this renovated heart will perform and for how long.

Sitting in the familiar blue chair looking out to an icy, windswept backyard. I just picked a red geranium from the pot by the window. I sniff it and think of spiritual writer Barbara Crafton's Geranium Farm.

She said most people don't think much of the geranium's scent. "They smell of dusty sunlight, of the tangy, spicy energy of life." I think so too. I enjoy their spreading blooms in our flower box hanging off the porch each summer. The deep red, black dirt and black shutters against the white stucco provide pleasing contrasts.

The flower is red, "not blood red," reminds Merton. Always liked that line from his journals. His point (I think) was that we don't need to call something as authentically red as a geranium "blood red." The color red of the geranium is powerful in itself.

Good lesson there for all of us. We are who we are—a soul loved by many and by God, however we define that. With great potential to love and receive love—and rich opportunities to use our gifts for others. That should be all we need to know. This surgery and all its components have helped move that truth to a more central spot in my life. Where it needs to be.

REFLECTIONS FOR WORK

We struggle with the changes that slam into our work lives. Big ones like downsizings, reorganizations, firings. Smaller ones like meetings that fail, colleagues who miss our points, interviews, reports, meetings and presentations which come up short. Opportunities that don't materialize. It's not easy to view these challenges as meaningless in the bigger picture of life and death. Everything is relative, of course, but we put our heart and soul into work. And when things get difficult, they take an emotional toll. We lose confidence. Self-doubts creep in.

I've referred to Nouwen's book, *The Inner Voice of Love*, before, the one where he wrote "spiritual imperatives" to himself each day as he struggled with all aspects of his life. The key takeaway for me with this writing was his point about "taking in love." When we feel disempowered in our work or transition, our initial impulse is to take action —work harder or change the strategy. Basically, do more to get more out of our work. Henri says "no"—do something different. Take something into our lives; take in love. How do we do that?

We all treasure the love we have in our lives. It's integral to all we cherish and strive for, but we have few practical ways of viewing "love" when making decisions or engaging the tasks of transition. Paula D'Arcy writes about placing herself into a play and God says, "Look at yourself, Paula. Really see yourself." She encourages us to respond to that important edict with valuable questions like, "Are my eyes and heart really open to the possibilities? Do I see what's right before me or only what I'm programmed to see? What would it take to look with eyes of love?"

That word again. How do we factor love into our situation?

Paula provides direction. "Life seems to follow this pattern: the journey unfolds as we live it out. My part is to let go with both hands and take the first step. The first step sets everything in motion. I think of Paul's journey through Greece and Turkey. Over a thousand miles on foot, searching for fertile hearts. Start walking, the Spirit demands. You're not alone. Love will lead the way. Take the first step. You are not alone."

PONDER

Whose love in my family or circle of friends can I really count on and how can that translate to practical help in my transition?

_____

_____

_____

_____

Who are the people I love and how is that love affected by
this transition? What difference does this make as I make
choices or find the courage to move ahead?

_____

_____

_____

_____

How can I really feel the love of people in my life so it can
inspire me and help me know my true self, my best self, my
strongest self?

_____

_____

_____

_____

What do I need to do to look deeply at this transition
through "eyes of love" and how can that make a difference in
my actions?

_____

_____

_____

_____

How do I define God's love and how do the examples of God's love in my life have an impact on this transition?

_____

_____

_____

_____

WHAT'S THE "NEXT THING" YOU WILL DO?

_____

_____

_____

_____

NOTES

Tom's Journal: At the End with Dad
6. BEING GRATEFUL

Dad's in such an impossible place—he isn't himself and he's not who he will be. The ultimate transition. And maybe the most painful. But there is something good and holy about this. And being here, close—helping him make it to where he's going.

Dad is frail, so skinny. But for me, his face is still Dad. And his smile tonight as I said goodbye, sobbing into his neck was an unexpected gift. I will remember it always. I forget what brought it on. It was fleeting on his face, lasting in my soul.

I thanked him for being a great Dad for 56 years—I've seen none finer and I've seen many. I told him he balanced praise and humility well in his fathering. That I hungered for more of his praise but now realized how much he valued humility and disdained arrogance. He wanted his sons to be sure they had the right perspective on their accomplishments and I think intentionally held back on his praise. My theory anyway.

There was a time when I thought I was chasing his love—but eventually figured out it was praise. I never doubted his love. One of his best lessons was not to call attention to yourself. If what you did had value, people will know.

I read in Ronald C. White's "American Ulysses: A Life of Ulysses S. Grant" that his mother demonstrated what a friend called "self-effacing Christian love." She felt that her children should not be praised no matter how well they did; praising the Lord for giving them the opportunity was what was required. That's a little extreme as I certainly remember Dad's affirmations.

But maybe he and Grant's Mom had a little something in common too.

REFLECTIONS FOR WORK

There could be many lessons in your new workplace and how you got there. Perhaps they fall into two groups: 1. Show gratefulness to those who helped you. 2. Begin to understand the new environment, including your new colleagues. Developing meaningful relationships in the workplace is a big part of job satisfaction as well as job success.

Think about the people who helped you along the way. Who were the ones supporting you, listening to you, brainstorming ideas with you, believing in you, referring you to others? How will you thank them? I think it's important to recognize what people did for you, not what they couldn't do. I often have unrealistic expectations of how people can help me. My desires are often out of line with reality. Hard to be realistic sometimes when we really need help.

Developing new relationships is integral to successful transitions. Use the skills you honed during your transition work, approaching people you didn't know with honesty, humility, genuine interest in their work, their organization, and their stories. You came armed with thoughtful questions, demonstrating you cared about them. You did some homework too.

These are the hallmarks of developing valuable relationships in your new workplace. And also the means to understanding the culture of the organization.

Edgar Schein said that an organization's culture is a deep phenomenon, mysterious, irrational and complex. But once you've gone deeper, you can better understand how to be successful.

I did consulting work for Fortune 40 Merck & Company at their corporate headquarters. In the early going, I observed that everyone seemed to be behind closed doors either producing or directing PowerPoint presentations. In every department, people had to build consensus at all levels for any idea or project by leading a formal PowerPoint meeting. I was curious how the real work got done! It occurred to me after some time, that this core aspect of the Merck culture reflected exactly what took place in their industry.

When any drug, therapy or device is introduced to the market, it had to proceed through an endless series of trials, studies, and protocols, before being sold to the public. Merck corporate was no different as new ideas, procedures and programs were launched in any department. It's not hard to come up with a list of qualities necessary for success at Merck. Besides the obvious PowerPoint, patience, persistence, working systematically and by the book, being a confident group communicator/facilitator and having solid research/evidence for your points make the list.

It's probably helpful to conduct a similar culture assessment in your new workplace.

PONDER

Who were the key people helping you in this transition? What did they do and how did they help?

_____

_____

_____

What lessons are you taking away from these relationships which will help you in your next transition?

_____

_____

_____

Who didn't you approach to help you in the transition and what were the reasons? Do you have any regrets about that? How could they help your career if you approached them now?

_____

_____

_____

What are your plans for developing new, meaningful relationships?

_____

_____

_____

_____

How will you get to understand the mystery and irrational of your new organization? How will that help you work more productively and effectively?

_____

_____

_____

_____

WHAT'S THE "NEXT THING" YOU WILL DO?

_____

_____

_____

_____

NOTES

Tom's Journal: Mom's Dying
7. PATIENCE IS NOT JUST A VIRTUE

I'm sitting by my Mom's bedside—her first day at the beautiful "Agrace HospiceCare" facility in Fitchburg, WI. This is her third time in hospice care, so I'm not convinced this is it. She's sleeping peacefully, still looking like my Mom, despite her deep wrinkles and drawn face. Beautiful. My thoughts turn to her mind and how as a young adult establishing myself in a career, her words seemed lightweight for my challenges. After listening faithfully, she would often say, "I guess we shall see what we shall see." "Oh, it will work out in the end" was also a favorite. My reaction was typically, "Thanks, Mom—I've got to get going."

Funny how perspectives change. At this stage of life and work, I fully value the importance of letting things play out or seeing what we will see. Waiting to see how things develop is useful. I only wish my Mom were still able to give me that cherished advice. Mark Twain said that he was amazed that as he aged, his father became smarter. Moms too.

REFLECTIONS FOR WORK

My Mom was not a scholar. She was smart; graduated from college in the 1940s; taught before she got married and raised four sons. Nevertheless, I always went to Dad for advice. In hindsight, the great teacher, I have come to appreciate Mom's wisdom.

Have you ever rushed into a project when you knew in your heart the timing wasn't right? Sometimes our egos believe we can handle the consequences. Other times, desperation or fatigue makes us take a job that may not really fit. Or we make a decision to undertake a new project without sufficient due diligence. We so believe in ourselves and our idea (not a bad thing) that we count on things working out.

As you adjust to your new workplace, there will be opportunities to "go the extra mile." Your boss and colleagues are counting on you to seize some of these opportunities. That's probably one of the reasons you were hired. It can be a difficult line to walk, however. This line between doing the job in the description and discovering additional ways to add value. And there are situations where you won't want to appear overly eager. Complex stuff. Taking your time, seeking counsel from people you trust and bringing these issues to prayer and reflection may be useful guidelines.

PONDER

Are you challenged by a decision which requires more information? What key person do you need to talk to or what kind of intelligence do you need?

What are the pros and cons of waiting longer before acting on an idea? Perhaps, allowing some development outside of your control to take place.

_____

_____

_____

_____

What opportunities do you see beyond your job description where you can add value? And how will you decide to pursue them?

_____

_____

_____

_____

WHAT'S THE "NEXT THING" YOU WILL DO?

_____

_____

_____

_____

NOTES

Tom's Journal: Mom's Dying
8. AND SO WE'RE BACK TO LOVE

The following quotes from people who wrote me after my Mom died provide a wonderful testimony to her love.

"Every time I saw H.A. I felt her love and interest in my life. I felt special and am sure my cousins did also as is evidenced by your gathering here in her honor."

"Your mom's "sparkle" is what I remember most about her. I will always remember your mom as one who could light up a room merely by her presence."

"Mom was an inspiration by putting everyone else- her parents, her children, neighbors, and relatives first in her life. She never expected anything in return for all the things she did for us. She was such a giving person, and we should all learn from this."

"I love to remember how good and safe I felt coming to see you, even though I had grown up so far away. Helen Ann, you have been a loving, steady presence throughout my life."

"Chuck talks about how welcome you always make him feel—he appreciates your warmth and kindness and loves to come visit you. I am so glad that Chuck can get to know Grandpa B through your stories. It's the next best thing to Chuck actually having met him."

"I also feel privileged for the time I've been able to spend with you, Grandma B......You're a good woman Grandma B, and you're a good mother who raised loving sons. You did your best, and that says a lot."

Life's River

By Mark Allen Budnik

A mother gazes into her baby's eyes

her love courses through him like a river

She nourishes him - he grows strong She comforts him -

he grows secure

She releases him -

he gains himself.

His life, too, flows like a river

deepening here, widening there,

nurturing new life along its length.

Meanwhile, Time - unyielding -

wears down all creation

Finally the mother looks one last time into her child's eyes -

the child sighs

and knowing the river is nearly dry,

releases a torrent of tears

vainly wishing to fill its banks

He comforts her -

she grows calm

He caresses her -

she gains acceptance

He releases her -

she floats briefly on the surface of life

and empties peacefully into the everlasting sea.

Illustration by Angie Tornes

REFLECTIONS FOR WORK

Love is an overused word in many situations. I've previously written about love using the old Beatles song, "All You Need Is Love" as context. We know Henri Nouwen has some wisdom on the topic as he writes that when we feel disempowered, we often fight to take outward action. What is truly needed is inward reflection. Stopping and pondering the love we have in our lives gives us the strength to move forward. When we know we are loved, we can be more our true selves. And we are stronger.

Although Mom was in hospice as her life faded, she kept "hanging on." My non-medical explanation was that her whole life long she was "easy to love," and all that love was keeping her with us.

In the work of transition, hanging on is sometimes all we can do. And that is often enough as in time, new strength from those around us, fresh resources and faith carry us forward. Love is the foundation of this strength.

I prize Daniel Hays' words in his memoir *My Old Man and the Sea.*

"Moms—what a thing!…You start out inside them so helpless that they breathe for you. You come out and they do practically nothing else but love you so much that the rest of your life seems like hard work."

If that's not the best description of my mom then I don't know what is. Maybe for your mom too. And maybe it's this kind of love which carried you through this challenging transition.

PONDER

Love, love, love…say it over and over; visualize it; twist it around and view it from many sides. Where is love in your life, both received and given?

_____

_____

_____

_____

How can you describe it? What are examples? In a sentence, how does it strengthen you?

_____

_____

_____

_____

What's your biggest difficulty in this transition? How can giving or receiving love help you?

_____

_____

_____

_____

How do you define God's love? How can it find a more prominent place in your life and in your transition?

_____

_____

_____

_____

WHAT'S THE "NEXT THING" YOU WILL DO?

_____

_____

_____

_____

Tom's Journal: A Cancer Journey
9. COUNTING ON WHAT'S REAL

Sitting in my favorite chair, looking out to a bleak, foreboding Lake Michigan. It's December so that's expected. Grey is the only color I see. Appropriate as I mull over my recent CT scan at Froedtert/Medical College of Wisconsin and await results day after tomorrow. I run through my usual preparation for this trial. Make a list of my blessings which there are many; be grateful for the 67 years of pretty great health I've already had; connect myself to the human race from the beginning of time and try and be as positive as I can about my mortality. Billions have faced the end of life and made the "big transition" before me.

So if my lymphoma is back and death awaits, I will try and accept that fate with grace. More than likely one of three things will occur, as I've reflected before. Scan is clear—go home to try and live with more gratefulness and love; lymphoma is creeping back—wait a while or begin to counter with some measure; or it's seriously back so serious measures need to be engaged—but there is hope and I still have some good life ahead of me.

In any case, Les my real doctor, and wife of 46 years will carry forth providing the love, laughs and relationship with which I've been blessed. My faith will still be around, maybe strengthening me more than ever. Somehow in love and mystery, God shows up in these times and the interior outcome is noticeably positive. Probably because when I get scared, God is my main resource.

REFLECTIONS FOR WORK

As we move into the transition of existing or new work, career, ministry or retirement roles, it can be helpful to reflect on what's true. Of course negative possibilities creep in. What if I don't prove myself in this new job? Maybe my boss won't view me as a top performer. Perhaps my commitment or focus won't be what's necessary for the organizational standard. Maybe I'm not as good as they think I am. It's possible other life priorities will interfere with the zeal and excellence the new place demands. What happens if I'm job hunting again in a couple of years? All possibilities. It's that kind of world.

But regardless of external happenings that you can't control, know that some things won't change. The qualities and resources you used to get where you are will likely be there again. Your strength. Your faith. Your God. Your significant friends, partner, spouse. There are good people in your corner—the ones who didn't and won't fail you. The commitment you have to find meaningful work. The desire to continue searching out and following your deeper call.

Know also that you have the capability to be resilient and adaptable in this new opportunity. It won't be perfect. But it has the potential to bring satisfaction, contentment and meaning. Count your blessings. You're glad to be employed and not out there looking.

PONDER

How do you let go of your disappointment at not getting your dream job and search for meaning in your existing or new reality?

_____

_____

_____

_____

Who are your best people to help you attain this healthy perspective?

_____

_____

_____

_____

Where does your faith, your spirituality, your God come into this process?

_____

_____

_____

_____

WHAT'S THE "NEXT THING" YOU WILL DO?

_____

_____

_____

_____

Tom's Journal: The Miracle of Oona
10. THE TRUTH OF THE WORK

She came out of nowhere. Not really but as our family has been around awhile without a grandchild, it felt that way. We kid that she rocketed in from the moon as she casts spells on everybody who sees her. And she seems wise and confident for such a newcomer! Crazy grandfather talk, huh. Oona Mae Harper Bachhuber found her way into our lives and the universe in the Autumn, 2016.

During the days leading up to and after her birth, I was reading James Martin's fine book, Jesus: A Pilgrimage.

He helps us understand how magnificent Jesus' parables are. They helped his simple, uneducated followers then and now understand God's truths in ways that are personal, meaningful. These stories are short, to the point, and use aspects of life to which people relate.

He cites his mentor, Daniel J. Harrington's definition: "A parable is a form of analogy that seeks to illuminate the complex reality of God's kingdom by appealing to something better known." The shepherd who leaves the flock for one lost sheep; farmer who sows seeds on different soils; woman who searches all day for her lost coin and when she finds it, celebrates with her friends, and the prodigal son who is welcomed home by the joyous father are well known to us. Martin suggests we try to write a parable to better understand their power. So I will try. And I'll use my new grandchild, Oona Mae, in the lead role. She is presently four months old but she will be four years all too soon. I hope she can help me convey an important belief I have about transitions.

THE PARABLE OF OONA AND THE BIRTHDAY CAKE

There once was a toddler named Oona. On her mom's birthday, she worked all day to make a drawing of a birthday cake for a present. She used all the crayons in her Crayola Box of 32. The drawing took up the whole page and as she was only four, it was a little hard to tell it was a birthday cake.

Mom's favorite cake had always been chocolate with buttercream frosting, which Oona's dad bought for her at the town's best bakery. He surprised her with it that evening and several friends stopped in to enjoy it. Oona also presented her drawing to her mom, who loved it and placed it on the floor with the other cards and gifts. Oona got to stay up with the party as everyone laughed, chatted and complimented the tasty cake. The perfect cake was the center of conversation with praise for its flavor, texture, and beauty.

After Oona was put to bed, she lay there puzzled about how her gift was received and a little sad about the evening. The drawing of the cake, other cards and gifts and of course the delicious buttercream-frosted cake each contributed to the party. But in the end, the cake from the expensive bakery was the highlight of the evening. A tiny tear dropped on her pillow before she shut her big blue eyes to fall asleep. Little Oona slept restlessly that night.

If only she had known that in her mom's heart it was her drawing of the cake, filling the whole page and using all 32 crayons, which made her weep with gratefulness before falling asleep. For her, it was the most beautiful gift she ever received. And she promised herself to tell Oona first thing the next morning.

REFLECTIONS FOR WORK

Often, the work in our jobs and the work of transition go un-acknowledged. With the former, we strive but many times struggle to call our boss's, clients', colleagues' and customers' attention to it. Of course, marketing our accomplishments is necessary for success. We need to know in our hearts that there is appreciation for our work even though it may not be expressed or acknowledged. However, we may not have a clue about the positive things people might say in other places. Or in future times. Complements we don't hear. There is also something intrinsically valuable about the work we may do, and the results may not show up.

Thomas Merton called this the "truth of our work" and it's sometimes not measurable—by sight, sound or research. In striving for new opportunities, we need to be visible to the people who can support us, refer us, hire us. Sure, we must use paper, web and personal meetings to call attention to what we do well and how it can positively affect new workplaces.

We need to understand in our souls that there are times when the reason we didn't succeed had zero to do with our performance. Someone else was there first; an insider got the advantage;

business went south; circumstances changed—lots of reasons. The value of what we did is still worthwhile to us, others and the universe. This truth doesn't make it hurt any less but it can help us continue the work. Merton also said, "and in the end, everything is saved by relationships." I like that. It tells me that we can positively impact people around us as well as be true to our vocation, while not succeeding as others define success. Maybe there's something reassuring in that.

PONDER

Think of a setback you've recently had. Reflect on what good still occurred.

_____

_____

_____

_____

Write down some things about the "truth of your work."

_____

_____

_____

_____

How can you continue to view your work in the framework of God's call or vocation?

_____

_____

_____

_____

WHAT'S THE "NEXT THING" YOU WILL DO?

_____

_____

_____

_____

NOTES

Tom's Journal: A Cancer Journey
11. NEW PERSPECTIVES HELP

Last week I was lost. Today, I am found; the cancer is losing the battle, for now. The CT-Scan is favorable. My face is not as red or dry. Energy is back. Hair continues to be there. And my beloved three kids are returning home this Thanksgiving to laugh, love and eat too much. The sun shines.

Ignatius teaches about consolation and desolation. These "motions" as he calls them, come and go as our life cycles change. When in consolation, I know I will be grateful, joyful—but also understand that this is life and it will not last. Prepare, pray. When in desolation, we need to embrace the pain as hard as that is. And work to be hopeful, surrendering to larger forces—and find strength in knowing it does not last. Prepare, pray.

Good lessons as I look to days ahead. And more transitions.

REFLECTIONS FOR WORK

The work involved in making a successful transition is rarely agreeable, much less enjoyable. But there are good things. As a counselor, I need to be more aware of both those realities as I encourage people to look at the positive outcomes:

❖ Excitement in discovering new truths,

❖ Confidence from overcoming adversity,

❖ New relationships with people who truly care,

❖ Support from those around you,

❖ Success—and a "reinvented self," as William Bridges says.

All true but when you're in the trenches, it's difficult to embrace that wisdom. It sometimes comes only after success is achieved. Transitions are characterized by highs and lows.

Ignatius of Loyola knew a thing or two about transition. He went from being a brave, romantic 16th century knight to a devout priest who founded the Jesuits. His Spiritual Exercises address the positive and negative thoughts which drive our hopes and fears when life changes.

When things are going well, celebrate and share the good news with those cool, key people around you. Highs get higher. But the work continues; and you should be inspired to do more. When darkness descends, these same key, cool people can be there to show you specks of light. They will remind you that dawn is coming. New, meaningful work is attainable. And there are opportunities for gratitude.

PONDER

Where are you in the cycle of consolation and desolation relating to your transition?

_____

_____

_____

_____

What message can you give yourself to help manage the situation?

_____

_____

_____

_____

Who are your cool, key people?

_____

_____

_____

_____

How can you pray and prepare for what might come next?

_____

_____

_____

_____

WHAT'S THE "NEXT THING" YOU WILL DO?

_____

_____

_____

_____

Tom's Journal: A Cancer Journey
12. HEAVEN ON EARTH

As I face these crossroads in my journey, I think about "heaven" — not as a place but as a state of being. I've always been cynical about the "place" idea. It seems simple-minded—of course, that may be just how I should think about it. Simply. In his Gospel (11:25-27), Matthew agrees. "Jesus said, "I thank you, Father, Lord of heaven and earth, because you have hidden these things from the wise and the intelligent and have revealed them to infants." Ah, to be childlike!

I wonder with hope that heaven will be beautiful. And I will know God's love and the love of others who are "there" in new, deeper ways. I realize I have nothing concrete or empirical here but the Carthusians' book ("Ever Ancient, Ever New: Praying with the Carthusians")with its obscure language seems to. At least for me.

"For us, space is only an accident and after time the most difficult to define and perceive while unions are substantial: that is to say constant and immutable. This is because there is within us vaster regions of the soul, where we no longer reason or argue, but see and taste and love. Live then, rather in these depths. They are the

kingdom of peace, because they are the abode of the God of peace. There you have the unchanging meeting place of our unions.

Actually, there is nothing really new, for we strive to live—unhappily not sufficiently—in that eternity, ever ancient, ever new. We lose in its depths our cares and troubles, for they are all only passing, whereas we are made for what is lasting and abiding."

One thing for sure, this disease is about me. Interesting. In so much of life, we need to be reminded that it's not about us. And we need to be prompted by others about this axiom. Other people have needs and priorities; they count. Well, I comfort myself a little tongue in cheek by saying, "If my cancer is back, then it is really about me." I will be in a more centralized position with family and friends—they have to give me new attention. Part of this of course is feeling their pity, which I despise.

But as I come to realize the grace, hope and strength which God provides, the pity becomes less—and turns to better things like support, care, love. All good. Beautiful. Grace, for sure.

REFLECTIONS FOR WORK

One of my favorite encouragements to people in transition is "Don't go it alone." It's too hard. We need the support, love and perspectives of others. Friends, mentors, coaches, teachers, counselors, colleagues, children, parents, grandparents, etc. And they do so much for us! Others care about us, believe in us, have faith that we can be successful; they want to go that extra mile for us. Amazing. These allies and angels want to refer us to others. They want to provide us a discussion on the key challenges of our field and how we can best address them. So we can most articulately present that in an interview. In a networking meeting. They want to listen to us and provide support, ideas. They want to introduce us to the "guy" who has an actual job. Really, they do.

But you know what? It's still about us. In transition, we're doing the hard work, the heavy lifting. Aching inside when we don't get the meeting, the job, the promotion. Only we can complete the assessments, research the possibilities, articulate our goals, compose the LinkedIn profile, construct the e-mails, complete the online applications, make smooth the elevator speech, prepare for the meetings, manage social media and messaging, find the courage to spend an extra hour, day, week, year to get to that place of new, meaningful work. Once we've arrived, new relationships and roles are challenging. The search for new meaning continues. Future transitions loom. Wow, that's a lot of work. For us.

In a way, I take pride in knowing that it's up to me. I'm the one who needs to make it happen. Nobody else can. Nobody else can take our place. Maybe we can find strength from that truth.

And maybe there is opportunity to grow our faith as well. As we know in our hearts, we often require a power beyond ourselves. I've said this before but it bears repeating. Dick Bolles says it well: "If you're in a transition and happen to have an old faith hanging in the closet, now is probably a good time to dust it off and bring it out."

I like that so much. I guess he's really saying it's not just about you—it's about faith in the people you place around you to help and faith in God too, however we personally define God. And God is always there. You need to look, sometimes look hard. To places far away and those deeper inside us. The eternal places where the Carthusian Monks look. So Dick Bolles, who just recently found his eternal resting place at age 90 (April 1, 2017), and the ancient monks named for the Chartreuse Mountains in the French Alps, come to our aid. They help us see God as resource and the Source—now, in work transitions and later in eternity. However we define that.

PONDER

What aspect of your transition is challenging you the most? And what can you do in your spiritual life to make a difference in meeting this challenge?

_____

_____

_____

_____

Name the parts of your faith you need to "bring out of the closet and dust off" so they can help you in this transition?

_____

_____

_____

_____

How is heaven or your ideas about eternity a part of your perspective in this transition?

_____

_____

_____

_____

Or if it isn't, do you want it to be? And if so, is there something you can do about it?

_____

_____

_____

_____

WHAT'S THE "NEXT THING" YOU WILL DO?

_____

_____

_____

_____

NOTES

Tom's Journal: The Miracle of Oona

13. EVERYTHING'S CHANGED

From the moment my daughter Libby announced that she was pregnant, I knew I'd be a wreck. My wife and I hadn't expected grandchildren when at age 40, our oldest daughter told us she and Seth were having a baby. I was excited but nervous for the health of my daughter and possible baby. Friends kept telling me their wonderful stories about being a grandparent. I got it. I always loved babies and kids—had four of our own. But also, one of the four (Christopher) was born with Downs Syndrome and died after open heart surgery at three months. Demolished us. Our other children have also experienced some difficult health challenges,

So I worried and prayed. I'm not big on intercessory prayer but when it comes to your kids, all bets are off. I prayed this prayer regularly and gave it to friends and family to pray.

> *Dear God of mercy, mystery and love, but most of all, God of precious, tiny life. We pray with our truest hearts and the most fervent faith we can find, for Lib and Seth to be strong and wise and love each other in deeper ways than ever before. And that their baby be safe and healthy now and throughout his or her whole life.*

So when the big day came, I was of course anxious. We joined Libby and Seth at the hospital and hugged them tightly as they left for the delivery room. I continued praying. After we knew the baby had arrived and the new parents were in the "getting acquainted" room with the baby, I went to the lobby to wait for Lib's sister, Em, arriving from Minneapolis. None of us knew anything yet about the baby or Lib. I spied the doctor across the lobby and ran to her. She saw me coming and said, "Everything is fine. Libby and the baby are great."

More welcome words have not been spoken. I hugged her, thanked her and as I was heading to the elevator, turned and asked— boy or girl? She laughed, "You'll have to ask Libby! I walked briskly to the room where my wife met me smiling and said, "She had a girl. And everything is good." I told her I knew the last part. Then Em called saying she was almost at the hospital. I went back downstairs, hugged my daughter and by that time she had a text from her sister. As we arrived back to the room, Lib, Seth and baby had just arrived.

Em walked into the room, spied this tiny, brand new perfect soul tucked in by her Mom. She gasped, "Oh, oh", ran to her sister's side in tears and hugged them both. Les and I watched this astonishing scene, smiling with wet eyes.

I've never had very strong faith in asking God for anything. But when it comes to the health of my loved ones, those doubts never mattered. And as I experienced the joy for this healthy, beautiful gift of a grand daughter which I had strenuously prayed for, I knew that my prayers would continue. A second one followed that evening.

Dear God of love, the gift of your beautiful Oona Mae to Lib and Seth, our family and the universe is perfect. Our hearts rejoice in her magnificence and weep in gratefulness. May she know your love her whole life long.

REFLECTIONS FOR WORK

Transitions sometimes end exactly the way we planned, or hoped. We get that great, new job. The promotion comes through. The volunteer work in retirement is meaningful. The project labored over makes a difference for the department. We attain the clarity we sought for vocation in our work. We find new work where gifts can be used to make a positive difference in an organization and others' lives.

So now maybe you're flying. And you're rightfully celebrating. You can reflect back on the work and the worry and know it was worth it. It's a chance to bask in this happy place.

It is also important to thank the people who helped you and to the God in whom you might have found wisdom, strength, persistence, love.

It's also important to be generous in your success and perhaps reach out to others who may be still searching. It's helpful to begin planning for your future development as there are still challenges ahead. You know there will be other transitions down the road.

And you will find meaning in them as well.

PONDER

Reflect on your success; what has helped you the most along the way?

_____

_____

_____

_____

What are you doing to celebrate the new meaning and satisfaction you're experiencing in your work?

_____

_____

_____

_____

To whom and for what are you grateful? How are you expressing your gratefulness?

_____

_____

_____

_____

What work is required now as you think about developing yourself in this new opportunity as well as thinking ahead to the next transition?

_____

_____

_____

_____

WHAT'S THE "NEXT THING" YOU WILL DO?

_____

_____

_____

_____

NOTES

CHAPTER 4:
IGNATIAN SPIRITUALITY
FOR WORK, SERVICE AND
RETIREMENT TRANSITIONS

A COMPLEMENT TO TRANSPIRATIONS

"In calling me to live my special qualities and characteristics, God planted deep in myself an original purpose—what my concrete self adds up to—and the desire to live that out."

–Ignatius of Loyola

This passage by Ignatius of Loyola (1491–1556), the medieval scholar and founder of the Jesuit order, appears on the title page of this book. When a friend Monica shared it with me, I knew I had found the perfect link between vocation and career development. Connecting that obscure call to "original purpose" and discerning "what my concrete self adds up to" is work, service and retirement planning--plain and simple.

Discernment is the ideal word to describe this process. The Webster's dictionary defines it as "bringing sound judgment to a decision" and as "applying spiritual guidance outside the bounds of reason and analysis to a course of action." We need both, of course, in navigating our way through complex work transitions. Identifying our inner feelings and finding the language to best describe our interests, skills, and values and how they can contribute to a better world is the central work in career, service, or retirement transitions.

Ignatius recognized this in the Middle Ages and integrated it into his spiritual teachings. This final complement to TRANSPIRATIONS applies Ignatian wisdom to career, service, and retirement transitions, hopefully making the book even more useful.

IGNATIUS: A BRIEF BIOGRAPHY

Ignatius of Loyola, the founder of the Jesuits and author of *The Spiritual Exercises*, was born Inigo Lopez de Onaz y Loyola in 1491, in the castle of Loyola, Spain. This was a period of great historical upheaval. New worlds were being discovered, and the Reformation was revolutionizing the church throughout Europe. As the youngest son in a family of seven sons and six daughters, Ignatius went into training to become a courtier and a soldier. He gambled, fought duels, and enjoyed the company of women.

During a battle, a cannonball shattered Ignatius's leg. Upon arriving home to recuperate, he found the battlefield doctors had set it badly. He was a vain man and had his leg re-broken and set again so it would be the same length as his other leg. He was concerned about how his pants would look—really! The operation and recovery were painful. After failing to obtain tales of romance and chivalry to distract him, he began reading books about the lives of Christ and the saints.

He was especially inspired by the deeds of Francis of Assisi and through them began to experience conversion. Realizing that discerning God's will was all-important in his life, he went to a monastery, made a full confession of his life's sins, and then traveled to Jerusalem, desiring to be in the places where Jesus walked, taught, and died. On his return to Manresa, Spain, he immersed himself in long vigils of prayer and poverty. He was ordained a priest and later formed the Society of Jesus, an order grounded in practices of social justice and spiritual formation. His vigils later became the foundation for his Spiritual Exercises, a guide written especially for lay people rather than people in religious life. He and his companions ministered extensively throughout Europe and traveled to the Holy Land, eventually winding up in Rome where Ignatius died in 1556. Today, the Jesuit Order (Society of Jesus) has over 16,000 members serving in a variety of positions and ministries including pastors, teachers, chaplains, doctors, attorneys, scientists and college/university executives.

THOMAS MERTON AND IGNATIUS LOYOLA

Trappist monk and social activist Thomas Merton referred to Ignatius's idea of "original purpose" in a compelling way, "I am obscurely convinced that there is a need in the world for something I can provide and there is a need for me to provide it" (*Thoughts in Solitude*, 1956).

Maybe the most well known Ignatian quote on the topic of obscure call is, "Go forth and set the world on fire." This can be both inspiring and daunting as we engage our work/service journey. His emphasis on the arduous process is reflected in the quote, "Act as if everything depended on you; trust as if everything depended on God."

Clearly, Thomas Merton had a lot to say about vocation. Although he is certainly a favorite of the author, readers deserve an explanation for his continual reference in this complimentary chapter to *TRANSPIRATIONS*. It is noteworthy that Merton engaged Ignatius's Spiritual Exercises before he began monastic life, finding them "tiring" but beneficial. He also researched the Jesuit Order as part of his discernment, initially attracted by the poetry of Gerald Manley Hopkins. But in the end, Merton writes, "There had never been any real attraction calling me to that way of life" which he thought was "geared to a pitch of active intensity and military routine which were alien to my own needs." (The Seven Story Mountain, 1948)

Although these two spiritual masters were separated by 300 plus years, the Atlantic Ocean, and a laundry list of theological ideas, they share a common, deep heart for the pursuit of vocation. Merton wrote about the significance of the "long interior struggle" to insure "there is no apparent constraint." (*The Intimate Merton-His Life from His Journals*, 1998) Merton struggled throughout his life to listen to God's call, even after he chose the religious life and the Trappist order.

At one point, he felt he was being called away from his Gethsemane home to a more autonomous situation in Central America, heading his own monastery. He was passionate about this opportunity and depressed when he learned that Rome turned down his request. The following quote reflects the excitement he felt about this prospect as well as, generally, how he pursued writing projects, learning opportunities, and mutually enriching relationships throughout his life. He wrote over 50 books and 10,000 plus pieces of correspondence over a twenty-seven-year period.

> "Either you look at the universe as a very poor creation out of which no one can make anything, or you look at your own life and your own part in the universe as infinitely rich, full of inexhaustible interest, opening out into the infinite further responsibilities for study, work and contemplation, interest and praise. Beyond all and in all is God" (*Choosing to Love the World: On Contemplation*, 1968).

Merton did not ignore the deep thinking which goes into meaningful discernment. His emphasis was similar to the Ignatian philosophy that interior work needs to be engaged on both spiritual and practical levels.

> "What is vocation? A call and a response. This definition does not say everything. To conceive the call of God as an expressed order to carry out a task certainly is not always false, but it is only true after a long interior struggle in which it becomes obvious that no such constraint is apparent" (*The Intimate Merton His Life from His Journals*, 1999).

Merton said he wanted to write a book "in which everything can go." I believe his life was that book.

BRINGING TOGETHER ELEMENTS OF
IGNATIAN SPIRITUALITY AND TRANSITION

Discerning our next work, service, or retirement opportunity involves searching deep areas of our life through reflection, solitude, and prayer while engaging in the hard work of career development. *TRANSPIRATIONS* helps infuse spiritual reflection into the transition process. The "Ignatian Model for Transition" can assist us to see how the four integrated elements of (1) Spirituality & Faith, (2) Vocation, (3) Decision-making/Discernment, and (4) Action toward Work/Service guide us in this journey toward new, meaningful work. The sections are numbered one through four as each one can sequentially build from the previous section. This is a way of viewing our progress through transition.

This model presents key questions to address and explore in each section while demonstrating flexibility to navigate the four major sections. It is a fluid, non-linear process, meaning we can move freely back and forth among the sections as we work towards clarity. Ignatius focused on these four elements in his teachings, and his spirituality is reflected in the questions for engagement.

Ignatian Model for Transition

CENTER FOR LIFE TRANSITIONS

What are ways for enriching my relationship with God so that I can acquire the confidence, inspiration and guidance I need to find the meaningful work/service for which I long? (Examen)

How do I with God's help, move from regret, doubt, uncertainty and even grief to productive activity? (Colloquy)

(1) Spirituality & Faith

How can I learn to listen more deeply to identify the "magis" (the more and greater) in the new work/service for which I long?

What gifts do I have which organizations, employers, my community and/or the world will value? (Examen)

How can I best pray about experiencing and exploring possibilities to which God may be calling me? (Prayer of Imagination)

(2) Vocation

What actions will help me find clarity, take steps forward and eventually attain new, meaningful work/service?

- Assessment
- Research
- Goals
- Preparation
- Execution
- Accomplishment

Action toward Work/Service (4)

What are my feelings (motions of the soul) and how is my spirit responding as I consider this transition?

How can I identify and then gather the graces (relationships, internal and external resources) which will bring me the support/guidance I need to successfully make this transition?

What central tasks do I need to accomplish in illuminating this transition to new, meaningful work/service?

Decision-making/ Discernment (3)

Copyright 2020. Center for Life Transitions, Inc
Original model design by Thomas Bobich,
LifeSHIFT-Work & the Christian Journey Retreatant
Modifications and narrative by Thomas Bachhuber

(1) SPIRITUALITY & FAITH

What are ways for enriching my relationship with God so that I can acquire the confidence, inspiration and guidance I need to find the meaningful work/service for which I long? (Examen)

How do I with God's help, move from regret, doubt, uncertainty and even grief to productive activity? (Colloquy)

Because faith and spirituality permeate our lives, it is reasonable to begin the work of transition with them. As Ignatius believed that we find God in everything, God is part of each facet of the "Ignatian Model for Transition." The Principles and Foundation of *The Ignatian Spiritual Exercises* teach that our central purpose in life is to live with God.

Ignatius wrote that it is important to develop our image of God as the groundwork for our spirituality. No matter how we envision God, we each have talents or gifts and tasks to accomplish in life. Ignatian Spirituality is about finding God in everything, while discerning how to best use our gifts to help a fragmented world. Understanding our individual spirituality and faith is complex, of course, so it is helpful to examine some attributes.

SILENCE AND SOLITUDE

Spiritual teachers tell us that silence and solitude are necessary disciplines to find the inner strength from God which enables us to make intelligent, enlightened decisions. Merton wrote, "Not all of us are called to be hermits, but all men and women need enough silence and solitude in their lives to enable the deep inner voice of their own true self to be heard at least occasionally" (*Thoughts in Solitude*, 1956). Our lives are busier and more complex than ever, making the case even more compelling to listen to the "still, small voice" inside of us.

IDENTIFYING OUR STRENGTHS

Transitions are always intimidating as we move from things we know and are comfortable with to things that are new and uncertain. Sometimes it can be helpful to focus on our successes in previous transitions in order to build confidence. In *Conjectures of a Guilty Bystander*, Merton wrote that we often avoid God in needy times because we feel uncomfortable with God and desire to be self-sufficient. He wrote, "Perhaps we are stronger than we think. Perhaps I would rather be guilty and weak in myself than strong in God whom I cannot understand."

This is a complex Merton idea, challenging us to embrace our faith even though it is a difficult process. Faith will make us stronger.

EXPLORING BIG QUESTIONS

Growing in our faith means investigating deep questions central to spirituality. This exploration helps us engage our interior to build a stronger, more intimate relationship with God and eventually find a new direction. Pondering "big questions" requires time alone and often the help of a counselor, coach, spiritual director, or good friend. Three rich Ignatian ideas followed by questions include:

❖ My deepest desire: What do I really long for (in my work)?

❖ Magis (Latin for larger, more, greater): What "greater good" would I like to have, achieve, or serve in my work?

❖ Generosity of spirit: Where can my gifts be best used to meet the needs of individuals, community, the world?

Engaging these questions requires us to be the deep people that Christian author Richard Foster refers to in his book, *Prayer*, "Superficiality is the curse of the age. The doctrine of instant satisfaction is a primary spiritual problem. The desperate need today is not for a greater number of intelligent people, or gifted people, but for deep people."

USING IMAGINATION

Balance is connected to meaning in much of life. We progress towards clarity by working and resting, and by using both our minds and hearts. Imagination is usually underutilized in the process. Ignatius knew that and made it an important part of his teachings on spirituality.

Ignatius heartens us in *The Spiritual Exercises* to have "living with God" as our life goal. And as we respond to the love we give and receive in life, we are better able to discover and live out God's call. This is the essence of the faith journey to Ignatius. One of many examples of Ignatius's use of imagination in scripture is to ponder the passage in Matthew's gospel where Jesus asks the two disciples who are following John, "What do you want?" Caught off guard, they reply with a question, "Teacher, where are you going?" Jesus says, "Come and see."

We are inspired to imagine Jesus asking us, "What do we want?" and then envision what Jesus is showing us when he says, "Come and see." This work with our distinctive imagination helps us discover the mystery of scripture by not just telling the story in our mind, but rather engaging the Spirit which allows us to personally encounter Jesus. The exercise works best if facilitated by a spiritual director as part of a larger program. Encounters like this allow us to not just observe but to actually experience scriptures.

Jesuit George Aschenbrenner wrote, "As we deepen our personal entry into the mystery, gathering over time into the interior, an intimate knowledge for which you are praying has begun. In this way, the mystery is happening right now, and you are more than an objective spectator. You are participating firsthand" (Stretched for Greater Glory, 2004).

Gaining direction toward new and meaningful work, service, or retirement requires a variety of approaches. Kathleen Norris, author of several spiritual works including, *The Cloister Walk*, provides a useful perspective:

"Imagination and reason are vital elements. Both bring us up against our true abilities and our limitations. But we've gotten ourselves into a curious mess in this modern world. We've grown afraid of imagination (except as a misguided notion of creativity granted to a few) and yet are less and less capable of valuing rationality as another resource of our humanity."

Imagination can be a powerful tool for all of us as we continue this journey toward new, meaningful work and service.

(2) VOCATION

How can I listen more deeply in identifying the "magis" (the more and greater) in the new work/service for which I long?

What gifts do I have which organizations, employers, my community and/or the world will value? (Examen)

How can I best pray about experiencing and exploring possibilities to which God may be calling me? (Prayer of Imagination)

Vocation, from the Latin, vocatio, means "call" or "summons" and appears frequently in the Bible. Biblical stories tell us of seemingly weak-kneed prophets like Moses, Isaiah, and Jeremiah (and women like Miriam and Deborah), called by God for "high stress, low paying jobs." They respond with excuses including shyness, not feeling respected, and speaking poorly. Of course, they eventually heed God's call and proceed to do mighty work. Examining what holds us back, where we hesitate, and why, is part of listening to our "call." These biblical characters have lessons for all of us. Ignatius spent the better part of his life searching for his vocation. Even after gaining approval from Rome to form his followers into the Society of Jesus (Jesuits), he faced countless decisions and challenges as the Society developed.

It could be naïve or simplistic to think we are searching for a single vocation when God may call us to many things. For example, we may use our gifts to be successful in our career so we can provide for ourselves, others, or family. While different gifts may help support a place of worship, a non-profit, or cause in which we believe. In his book *God Finds Us*, Jim Manney provides a profound outlook on vocation:

"Beneath the love of money, possessions, honor, and pride, we will find what we really want. And here is Ignatius's great insight. When we find what we really want, we find what God wants, too. It's a pretty remarkable idea, so I'll say it again: when we discover what we really want, we discover what God wants, too."

OBSTACLES

Ignatius encourages us to reflect on the source of any resistance we may be feeling when contemplating change. As we begin to explore new possibilities in our own work, service, or retirement, our first reaction is often fear, then maybe unsuitability, or even unworthiness. These reactions disempower us, resulting in malaise or immobility. We may need to reflect more deeply on why we believe it is important to change our work lives. We also need to examine our fears as part of this reflection. Fears typically begin to dissipate once we know what we want to do. Getting a plan together can be the first step.

Naming, claiming, and thereby taming fears can be helpful. Dr. William Sneck, SJ (*Struggling with Shame, Anger, Guilt*, 2004) uses this Ignatian wisdom in his teaching. Being honest that we have fears and then specifying what they are helps us better manage them. We are then able to discover resources for help. And move ahead.

Hindsight is the great teacher. Throughout our work life, circumstances often dictate why we choose certain directions. We frequently make decisions based on poor or incomplete criteria. Maybe we chose a college because the campus was pretty or it's far enough away from home. We selected a course of study because we liked a professor or it promised more job choices. We took a new position because it paid well or switched fields because our significant other moved to a new city. But seldom do we search our hearts for what is really important. Maybe this time is different.

DIFFERENT KINDS OF CALLS

Call can be a complex, deep message, like a complete change in applying our gifts to a career, or it can be in a common, everyday aspect of life, like reaching out to a homeless person on the street while taking a walk. Call can be discovering an aspect of nature which might nourish our spirit or gaining a fresh perspective on a social issue from a new friend.

There are some helpful guidelines for us in the small, valuable book, *Listening Hearts, Discerning Call in Community*. The writers make these observations about God's call:

❖ God calls each of us, and there are a variety of calls.

❖ No one call is inherently better or higher than any other.

❖ A call can be big or small; a new direction in life or a new way to speak to someone.

❖ There is not necessarily a call from God in every decision; God is not always giving us specific guidance.

❖ A call from God might lead us to a new career but not necessarily total commitment to a career. We are called to minister to people outside of career.

❖ A sign of a call is a certain restlessness, a certain dissatisfaction with the way things are, a sense of wandering, yearning, a being at a crossroads.

❖ Call usually involves service or benefit to others—it's probably suspect if it doesn't.

❖ The fruits of call may be a long time coming; indeed, we may never perceive them; sometimes the fruits even manifest themselves even after our deaths.

❖ A task or undertaking can be good without being what we are called to do. To be doing what is good can be the greatest obstacle to doing something even better.

❖ A call doesn't usually come with a "roadmap" or pre-planned process; our freer faculties are required, using intelligence, creativity, sensitivities, and love.

It is evident that call can take many forms and is a slippery, expansive idea. It is a profound appeal from something both within and beyond ourselves—often guiding us to new opportunities which may initially seem foreign but which we have always known in our heart. Vocation can also be elusive because it may be using the gifts we have always had but which may need to be rediscovered, developed, or enhanced. The concept of gifts is quite concrete, however. Think about where our interests (what we like), values (what we care about), and skills (what we're good at) lie, and how they intersect. Determining how and where to best use them is another challenge in this journey where again, guidance from coaches, counselors, or spiritual directors can make a difference.

FINDING OUR TRUE SELF AND PATIENCE

Thomas Merton wrote about the "true self" which is central to the idea of vocation. Matt Emerson articulates this emphasis in his article, "Merton and the True Self" (*The Ignatian Educator*, 2013). He wrote, "It is awakening the true I, the Christ within, and dying to the vaporous and destructive ego created by fear." As we focus away from the ego and on the "true I," we are encouraged toward the new, meaningful work we desire and deserve.

When we are expected to provide necessary earnings for self or family, of course, we may not have the comfort or time to search for deep ideas or take on a reflective exploration of vocation. We may have to buy some time by securing employment to meet more pressing needs while continuing to pray and work toward that more meaningful, obscure call. Knowing that patience and priorities are part of the journey can be comforting as this road turns and twists.

At some point, we must come to believe that full-sized questions—often unanswered for now will characterize this discernment time and may be answered later. As Rainer Maria Rilke wrote:

> *"Be patient toward all that is unsolved in your heart and try to love the questions themselves,*
>
> *like locked rooms and like books that are now written in a very foreign tongue.*
>
> *Do not now seek the answers, which cannot be given you because you would not be able to live them.*
>
> *And the point is, to live everything. Live the questions now.*
>
> *Perhaps you will then gradually, without noticing it, live along some distant day into the answer."*

— *Rainer Maria Rilke*

NOTES

(3) DECISION-MAKING/DISCERNMENT

What are my feelings (motions of the soul) and how is my spirit responding as I consider this transition?

How can I identify and then gather the graces (relationships, internal and external resources) which will bring me the support/guidance I need to successfully make this transition?

What central tasks do I need to accomplish in illuminating this transition to new, meaningful work/service?

The weighty question, "What do I really long for?" is a key decision-making tenet in Ignatian Spirituality. It deserves deep examination of our true feelings. This does not mean a quick "what feels right," but neither does it mean a prolonged self-analysis which can often lead to paralysis. Ignatius refers to positive and negative "motions of the soul" that flow in and out of us. This good and evil, positivity and negativity, constantly pass through our "interior", causing both hope and fear to come and go.

"Consolation" is Ignatius's term for the presence of the good, true spirit providing a time to be thankful, hopeful, and purposeful in transition. We find encouragement and progress in transition. Ignatius uses the term "desolation" for the absence of the good, true spirit or the presence of the negative, false spirit which can cause us to be discouraged, immobilized, and even depressed. Ignatius advises us to make decisions when we are in consolation and avoid them in desolation. Modern psychology supports his wisdom that ideas broaden with positive emotions and narrow with negative. We are better able to solve problems, help others, and gain clarity in life choices when in this positive frame of mind and spirit.

In *The Inner Voice of Love*, the theologian Henri Nouwen tells us that the main question we should be asking is whether we are living with or without God. Every time we do something for our own affirmation or acceptance, God is not present. When we do something for the glory of God, we will find God's peace and rest in our hearts.

Few of us make even serious decisions with life changing consequences using devoted time for prayer, meditation, or reflection. Soul work often gets short shrift. Human nature unfortunately pushes against our true being, so we can get on with those life tasks which we feel are more important. This is a work in progress, of course, and taking structured time for solitude, silence and reflection can pay dividends in successful transition decisions.

FIND COUNSEL AND USE YOUR IMAGINATION

Going it alone while in transition is never preferable and getting support has been a message throughout TRANSPIRATIONS. Talking through decisions with a trusted professional or caring person is "required" in any work/service transition. Ignatius felt that keeping our decisions from others is a sure sign that the "evil or false" spirit is in control. In the book, *What's Your Decision? How to Make Choices with Confidence and Clarity*, the authors emphasize that "decision-making is inherently collaborative." This collaboration allows us to further our loving relationships with important people—and with God. These authors also provide concrete examples of using imagination in decision-making:

❖ Try on your proposed choices for size—really think and feel what it would be like if you choose that path. Go over specific tasks, roles, people, challenges, and joys in your head and heart.

❖ Imagine looking back at the decision from the end of your life. Are the values you hope to hold at the end of your life the same or close to those you are using to make this decision?

A friend of mine used to raise the rather menacing question, "How long are you going to be dead?" when I was mulling over a decision. That sometimes boosted me to take a risk and try something new or daring.

Theresa of Avila encourages us to use our imagination and dream big. She wrote, "It is a great help to high aspirations because often our actions begin with our thoughts and dreams. It is not pride to have great desires" *(The Interior Castle, 2007).*

Henry David Thoreau says that our dreams should be beautiful, like castles in the air, but they also need a foundation under them. As is emphasized throughout this chapter, imagination along with practical considerations are necessary for success.

TIMING AND NETWORKING

It's rarely an optimal time to make important decisions. It's especially difficult when going through tough stretches at work. Even though we may not be able to move to a new situation—job, employer, organization, city—it may be ideal to begin making plans. Also, the pain of a situation can encourage us to make small, positive changes where we are. Deliberate decision making is thoughtful, patient, and uses available resources around us. Research is "the hard work" of decision-making, requiring time, planning, and support. This can be done anytime and includes print and web resources as well as that all-important but usually misunderstood, networking.

True networking is authentic, honest discussion. Both people we know, and those we need to know, are rich sources of support and information. The key to helpful networking is deep, creative research; then forming that intelligence into knowledgeable, penetrating questions—for ourselves and people in discussion. In that way, meetings are mutually beneficial with each participant giving value to each other.

KEY CONSIDERATIONS IN RESEARCH AND DECISION-MAKING

Using print, media, and informational interviews in the research process leading to intelligent choices about career, service, and retirement.

❖ Find information about each opportunity and get varied, informed perspectives from key people.

❖ Follow the principal of "translating information to intelligence." Information is static but as your research is translated to specific questions and observations, it becomes crucial intelligence for meetings, interviews, and conversations. For example, if you learn that an organization increased its traffic in a season, you could ask a question like, "What changes did you make in marketing that increased visitors to your site?"

❖ In seeking clarity in your career, service, or retirement goals (or comparing options/opportunities), you're encouraged to identify key criteria for each choice, placing numerical values (e.g. 3-High, 2-Average, 1-Low) on each criterion. Compare how you rated various opportunities.

   a. Position of God, faith, spirituality in the work itself and/or workplace

   b. Work fit with personal interests, strengths, values

   c. Organizational culture/uniqueness

    d. Personality and spirituality of co-workers, colleagues, supervisors

    e. Potential for varied assignments, advancement, new opportunities

    f. Compensation, benefits, perks

    g. Work/Life balance

    h. Position security/stability

    i. Opportunity to be your authentic self

❖ Use clear, concrete language in describing work, service, or retirement choices. The emphasis should be on action verbs like "negotiate, counsel, repair, renovate, create" which create positive images in the minds of the reader or listener in your meetings.

❖ Use spiritual disciplines like keeping a journal, prayer, meditation, nature, sacraments, music, "lectio divina" (deliberate, repetitive, reflective scripture reading), and time in retreat/sacred environments to ensure your spirit is engaged in this process.

❖ Be responsible for sharing your decisions with key "stake-holders," e.g., spouse, partner, children, mentor.

London School of Business Professor, Herminia Ibarra, author of *Working Identity: Unconventional Strategies for Reinventing Your Career*, brings a helpful conclusion to this challenging topic of decision-making:

"Our work identity is not a hidden treasure waiting to be discovered at the very core of our inner being. Rather it is made up of many possibilities: some tangible and concrete, defined by the things we do, the company we keep, and the stories we tell about our work lives; others existing in the realm of future potential and private dreams."

Ibarra encourages us to gradually expose ourselves to new worlds, relationships, and roles. As we travel this journey with the love of people around us and a faith in something deeper, stronger, and smarter, there is hope that new work with new meaning can be discovered. We remember again Richard Foster saying that the world does not need more intelligent or gifted people, but rather deeper people. "They urge us to be the answer to a hollow world." And deeper people who maintain faith, hope, and love in their lives, do extraordinary things.

(4) ACTION TOWARD WORK/SERVICE

What actions will help me find clarity, take steps forward and eventually attain new, meaningful work/service?

- **Assessment**
- **Research**
- **Goals**
- **Preparation**
- **Execution**
- **Accomplishment**

These six components provide structure for accomplishing the important tasks of a successful transition to new, meaningful work. They are addressed in several parts of TRANSPIRATIONS. *Assessment* is both understanding and communicating our essential qualities (interests, skills/abilities, values, experiences) in clear, concrete, credible language. *Research* is doing the important work to gain awareness of organizations and opportunities. *Goal setting* is a process of "putting the pieces together" and results in concise statements of where we want to go. It is critical to success as it allows us to match ourselves intelligently and persuasively to organizational needs. It is maybe the hardest work and often given insufficient effort by most. We can also find inspiration once we articulate our dreams. *Preparation* is about doing your homework in optimizing your knowledge of the organizations, opportunities and people you will be approaching. Your confidence will grow in leaps and bounds as you practice for these engagements, better understanding (and articulating) how your gifts can make a difference. *Execution* includes the multiple ways we contact people, places and openings/opportunities with paper, technology, and in person. Actively using *LinkedIn*, other social media, resumes, emails, and networking are all part of this work. *Accomplishment* is the satisfying outcome and joyful reward in achieving new work/service.

TAKING ACTION

Ignatius strongly believed that God is found in acting—in the doing not just in the process and prayer that precede work, service, and retirement. This concept was integral to his genius. So, it is not surprising that this is also wisdom for successful transitions. Herminia Ibarra highlights the importance of engaging real experience anyway we can--paid or unpaid, short or long term. This is where real education takes place. "We learn who we can become not so much through self-analysis but rather through exploration, experimentation, and experience" *(Working Identity, 2003).*

Ignatius also helps us here through his principle of "changeable election." That means that decision-making is not irrevocable and almost always has possibilities that can take us in different directions. In his book *God Finds Us*, Jim Manney writes, "St. Ignatius recognized that God's will is not a precise blueprint, but neither is it a vague 'whatever you want' blank check." There is a general understanding that our mission on earth is to love and serve God and neighbor with each of us having both opportunity and responsibility to determine how to best do that. The desire to discern and carry out that work and service can happen at any juncture or throughout our lives.

Ignatius trusted that the soul needs activity in the same way the body requires physical training for health. His spiritual exercises of prayer and meditation, intended to help people connect to their faith in imaginative ways, are characterized by several principles that are also helpful in taking successful actions toward meaningful work and service.

NOTES

Principle of Ignatian Spirituality:
Ignatius believed the soul needs exercise for growth.

Transition to Work/Service:
We need to engage in "work" (exercise) to be successful, i.e. assessment, research, goal setting, networking and preparation for job seeking.

Principle of Ignatian Spirituality:
Ignatius believed spiritual directors/mentors/companions in the spiritual formation process can enhance meaning and outcomes.

Transition to Work/Service:
We need counseling/coaching to provide support, structure, guidance, and inspiration in our transitions. The mother of the iconic children's writer and performer Mr. Rogers gave him sound advice early in life: "When you are scared, look for the helpers. You will always find people who are helping."

Principle of Ignatian Spirituality:
Ignatius teaches that when we are discouraged or feeling desolation, we should increase our prayer and penance—reach out and do something positive. Even while feeling disempowered, we can think of situations where accomplishing even a small act of self-denial or kindness to another has freed our spirit from its negativity. Doing this provides evidence that we still have strength—and may be able to accomplish even greater things. Fear is a common reaction to many situations where our physical, emotional, or spiritual welfare appears threatened. Ignatius advises us against decisions made out of fear. We need to gather support around us and have faith that we have the resources and inner strength to overcome the fear.

Transition to Work/Service:
We encounter discouragement and even depression through uncertainty in our work direction, failure in the job market, rejection
by employers, and disillusionment in retirement. We need to acknowledge these feelings, confront them, and seek people to help.
Parker Palmer, spiritual writer and speaker, tells us that fears are
natural when we are facing transition but it is important to "not be
our fears" (*Let Your Life Speak*, 2000).

We need to find other places of strength. It's foolish to tell ourselves (or someone else) not to be afraid. We cannot just stop fear.
When Jesus appeared to his disciples walking on the Sea of Galilee,
he said, "Do not be afraid, have courage. It is I." He was offering
them a better option: Himself! "It is I!" We need to follow Parker's
guidance and find that other "place of strength" so fear does not
overcome us.

Principle of Ignatian Spirituality:
"Examen" is an Ignatian principle and practice of reflecting deeply
on our life as "sacred history" and identifying where God is present. And where we perceive God to be absent.

Transition to Work/Service:
We need to engage in introspection and assessment on a regular
basis, reviewing experiences, gifts, and opportunities to discern
how they are useful in determining new direction.

Principle of Ignatian Spirituality:
"Magis" (Latin for "greater" or "more") is part of a phrase Ignatius used, "Ad majoram Dei gloriam"—for the greater glory of God. Ignatius believed people should live their lives with this purpose in mind.

Transition to Work/Service:
We all desire opportunities to use our finest gifts—where interests, skills and values intersect—to the benefit of individuals and organizations no matter what our profession or field. When we do this, life has rich meaning and work becomes spiritual.

Principle of Ignatian Spirituality:
"Colloquy" is a conversation with God or Jesus, and Ignatius instructs us to speak as a friend or servant. This opens a full range of possibilities to honestly share both concerns and joys as with a close friend or colleague. As a servant speaking to one's master, one can ask for any variety of things: guidance, strength, wisdom, and comfort.

Transition to Work/Service:
Ignatius is not clear on how to listen for a deeper reply or interaction during the colloquy. Keeping a journal can help us engage in this conversation. Writing a journal about the ups and downs of our transition can be therapeutic, healing, and inspirational. The monk in the book, *The Little Monk*, uses his journal as his fourth counselor—church, friends, and prayer being the other three.

A WORD TO MY COMPANIONS: OLDER ADULTS IN WORK/SERVICE TRANSITION

People "retire," "re-fire," and "re-hire" at many ages. A common piece of advice is to "retire" for something not just from something. This is especially true if one desires to pursue and make gains on the ever elusive "meaning" in life. My friend Jim tells me that as we get older, we must not go quietly into the night—a variation of Dylan Thomas's phrase, "do not go gently into the good night." I have been "wrestling" with him on this one. I also like charging into activities new and old as long as health, time, money, and priorities permit. But also—I think we need to stop and smell the roses. And only through pause, prayer and silence will we glimpse truth, and be grateful for the blessings in our lives. We're both working on it.

Wendy Lustbader, author, speaker, and expert in the field of aging, provides this wisdom:

"The shock of realizing we have gotten older often turns some-day into now. We suddenly locate ourselves further on the trajectory between birth and death, and a bolder spirit overtakes us… something spurs us to recognize that our former purposes do not suffice, and we cannot wait any longer to follow our heart's desire (*Life Gets Better*, 2006).

So here we are again—back to our central theme of vocation. Calling. Searching. Discerning how to use our gifts and find meaningful, new work or service. It is never too late to discover the opportunity, organization, people, or role that makes a difference in the world—and enriching our soul in the process.

Some simple guidelines include:

❖ Begin thinking about and planning for "something else" before you retire. That can include concrete opportunities that use your gifts or at least make a commitment to exploring new possibilities.

❖ Of course, networking and relationship building is critical to this process. We have much to gain by getting out and talking to people about our ideas, dreams, and possibilities. But it is not easy, requiring assistance and gentle beginnings. Remember, networking is nothing more (or less) than asking people thoughtful questions about their work and allowing that process to evolve.

❖ Get a friend, coach, advisor, mentor, or spiritual director to help, guide, support, listen. The work of transition is too demanding to go it alone.

❖ Talk and write about the meaningful work, service, or volunteer possibilities to which you aspire. Identifying clear language around your thinking can help translate the abstract to concrete. And it is critical for people to understand you as you move through this process.

❖ Listen to our guide, Dr. Ibarra—experiment, explore, examine, try out. She says most of us "are more likely to act our way into a new way of thinking than to think our way into a new way of acting." (**Working Identity**, 2003) And recall that Ignatius's genius was finding God in the action we take.

❖ Back in 1987, business writer Jack Falvey said we need to "get out in the rain where it's cold and wet—that's where lightning strikes." We often learn, discover, and connect when we are uncomfortable—where people and places are new. And Jack also says "foxhole religion" can be useful. When you're in a "battle," find that deep, divine place beyond yourself where there is comfort, strength, even guidance. Meditate. Pray. Go on retreat.

Parker Palmer in his book, *On the Brink of Everything: Grace, Gravity & Getting Old*, speaks to the challenge of discerning vocation at later life. He puts a bow on the topic with his usual eloquence and depth:

> "Age itself is no excuse to wade in into the shallows. It's a reason to dive deep and take creative risks. For over a decade I have been reflecting on questions about aging and vocation. During most of that time, my key question was one I've heard others ask: 'As I get older, what do I need to let go of and what do I want to hang onto?'
>
> But somehow, that question didn't work for me—it did not open unto paths I wanted to walk. After talking with friends and colleagues, I'm now asking, 'What do I need to let go of and what do I want to give myself to?' Looking at what I want to give myself to takes me to places where I find energy, abundance, trust, and new life. The paths open onto paths with a heart."

There is a connection between letting go of things and giving yourself to things. You certainly may need to reprioritize some behaviors or practices in order to reach something better, richer, and deeper. When you take the time and energy to first clarify and then bring newly discovered, nurturing opportunities into your life, all things are possible. Meaningful work/service at any stage of life is that beautiful! Amen.

IGNATION SPIRITUAL WORK: ACTIVE REFLECTIONS

The following active reflections may be helpful as you discern vocation and new, meaningful work at any life stage. They were developed from Ignatius's Spiritual Exercises as interpreted by David L. Fleming, SJ in the book, *Draw Me into Your Friendship: A Literal Translation and Contemporary Reading of The Spiritual Exercises*. This work appears in *Moment by Moment: A Retreat in Everyday Life*, by Carol Ann Smith, SHU and Eugene F. Merz, SJ.

These five Active Reflections are for individual use. *The Spiritual Exercises* in total are always given or facilitated by a trained Spiritual Director over an extended retreat or period of time.

ACTIVE REFLECTION 1

Reflect on the transition you are facing and write both the positive and negative "motions of the soul" which are taking place inside of you.

Positive/Consolation:

_____

_____

_____

_____

_____

Negative/Desolation:

_____

_____

_____

_____

_____

What negative thoughts might be serving as obstacles as you plan this transition?

_____

_____

_____

_____

_____

Name one or two external sources or resources that you might turn to for strength, direction, comfort:

_____

_____

_____

_____

_____

How will you access these sources or resources and describe how you believe they might help?

_____

_____

_____

_____

_____

ACTIVE REFLECTION 2

Spiritual Exercise 97:

"Those of whom are of great heart and set on fire with zeal to follow your inner call will not only offer themselves entirely to labor for such a mission but will act against anything which would make their response less total."

Make a statement or two about your passion for the option or opportunity under consideration and how this could be used to help you either clarify what you need to do or take action:

_____

_____

_____

_____

_____

ACTIVE REFLECTION 3

Spiritual Exercise 315:

"The good spirit, however, strengthens and encourages, consoles and inspires, establishes a peace and sometimes moves to firm resolve. To lead a good life gives delight and joy, and no obstacle seems to be so formidable that it cannot be faced and overcome with God's grace. The good spirit thereby continues an upright person's progress in responding to God's continuing invitation."

Name the "good spirits" in your life. They might be people, ideas, exercise, music, beauty in nature. How do they help you move forward in your life to know love and to stay strong?

_____

_____

_____

_____

_____

_____

_____

_____

_____

ACTIVE REFLECTION 4

Spiritual Exercise 139:
"I ask for the gift of being able to recognize the false and negative lights...and for the help not to be led astray."

Spiritual Exercise 325:
"The evil or negative spirit often behaves like a spoiled child. If a person is firm with children, children give up petulant ways of acting. So, our tactics must include firmness in dealing with this spirit in our lives."

How may have you been misled, misinformed, or deceived—or what mistakes have you made on a previous life/work decision? What lessons did you learn?

_____

_____

_____

_____

Have there been situations where selfishness or self-centeredness has gotten in the way of making a good decision or being the person you what to be? In hindsight, how might you have better managed the situation or decision?

_____

_____

_____

_____

_____

ACTIVE REFLECTION 5

Spiritual Exercise 329:

"When we are trying to follow God's loving invitation, we will find that the good spirit tends to give support, encouragement and oftentimes even a certain delight in all our endeavors."

Describe a time when you were engaged in any project or piece of work when you felt inspired and/or pleased by the work itself or the outcome.

_____

_____

_____

YOUR NEXT THING

Baptist Minister and WWI chaplain, Oswald Chambers, said that when things appear complicated and confounding, it is because we have partial visions. He advises we step back, reflect or pray...we will know what our "next thing" is.

Successful transitions are a series of "next steps." It may be important to take a step, maybe any step.

WHAT MIGHT YOUR "NEXT THING" LOOK LIKE?

_____

_____

_____

_____

NOTES

EPILOGUE

With the darkness of 2020 thankfully in our rearview mirror, I try to find specks of light---and hope for the future. The pandemic still rages, and I am reminded that we are not all in this together. More than two million have died worldwide and tens of thousands suffer from Covid's effects. Countless populations are not receiving the healthcare they need and deserve.

My family has minimal problems here on the home front, so far. My daughter, her partner and my granddaughter have been sheltered here for going on a year, with more months ahead. There have been adjustments and challenges to be sure, but I will always cherish this time of family closeness. Beloved spouse of almost 50 years, Leslie, constantly reminds me of this truth. Welcoming each morning with a beaming, now four-year old Oona Mae is a matchless blessing.

This previous year also delivered us a highly contentious election, an insurrection on our nation's capital, necessary and new awareness of endemic racial and economic injustices and a damaged economy where people fortunate enough to retain their jobs and/or businesses continue work from home.

It is a serious understatement that life has changed markedly from when *TRANSPIRATIONS* was first published in 2018.

I also reflect on how fast time has and continues to go by, like a high-speed train where the scenery from the window is blurry.

Personally, my renovated heart now has twelve plus years on it, with another surgery in the offering. My lymphoma has been in remission for almost seven years and I am hopeful for many more.

No guarantees. My Dad's been gone for 13 years, Mom a little over three. I miss them all the time. And the infant granddaughter, Oona Mae, is now a fully engaged "4 girl"--thinking deeply, reading madly, and directing most family matters. I have some awareness of new transitions down the road. They are coming. And some will be very challenging.

Poet and essayist, Jane Hirshfield, advises, *"Everything is changing...Everything is connected...Pay attention."* And so, I will try. And I hope you will too. Our old friend Tom Merton teaches about *"pointe vierge"* (virgin point) and like you, I continue to be at several in my life/work. These ongoing, holy moments between night and dawn "when birds awake, become fully themselves and even fly" (Merton says with a wink) characterize our transitions.

My life continues to be vital but death and what's beyond is not that far away. Who knows when? Or where? At 72, I am also finding that cherished loved ones are getting sick or just old and leaving this planet in disquieting numbers.

While we are here, however, I believe we continue to encounter "pointes vierge," and we can choose to work through these transitions, remaining open to God's grace. Or we can try to be content with the status quo, often persisting in lethargy and related distress. And struggle with our "untrue selves." The status quo can be extremely comfortable. These are not easy decisions; I know from experience.

I am of course hoping for growth in my faith and spirituality. This kind of growth requires sweat. All good things do. From the introduction to this book, you know I cherish the Gospel story from Mark 19 where a father and his epileptic son pursue Jesus into a busy marketplace. He fights through protective disciples who do not want to bother Jesus.

Parents understand what is happening here as the father desperately fights for his child's health. He makes it to Jesus and is immediately asked about his faith. In front of God and everyone in the marketplace, the father shares his vulnerability by responding, "Lord, I believe; help me with my unbelief." A central measure of our journey seems to be wrestling with these non-beliefs. I resonate to the father's honesty, however, and so does Jesus. The child is healed. I find hope in both this process and poignant outcome. And this characterizes my faith—in a nutshell.

Life certainly has its ups and downs; we continually get knocked around. So, over and over I must learn this truth—that no matter what the challenge or crisis, my life is still precious and promising. I am blessed with people who love me and who I love. There are always possibilities which offer meaning and delight in the face of danger and uncertainty. Hope is continually alive. My faith journey is best walked at night where it is less reassuring and full of ambiguity. Death is guaranteed some time, every time, all the time and for everybody. And preparation for it is essential.

For me, God is real in unknown, misunderstood, and mysterious ways but also in personal and sustaining ways too. I am grateful for a mission and a ministry; an obscure call—and my heart will always hunt for what I need and will rest in what I have.

Ignatius of Loyola asks me to *"live out my special qualities and characteristics, identify what my concrete self adds up to."* And be faithful to the original *"purpose which God planted in me."* I will carry on this passage. Jesuit Alfred Delp facing execution in a Nazi prison camp says it with astonishing elegance:

"We regain faith in our own dignity, our mission and our purpose in life precisely to the extent that we grasp the idea of our own life flowing forth within us from the mystery of God." (*Alfred Delp, S.J. Prison Writings,* 2004)

It is the "mystery" that makes our journey so challenging, but maybe with a "breakthrough" now and then, so rewarding as well. I hope to keep striding forward in this amazing life. With lots of help from inside, outside, and beyond.

And like Merton's birds at dawn, maybe someday, I will even fly!

How about you?

TRANSPIRATIONS

TRANSPIRATIONS

APPENDICES

Prayer at Beginning of LifeSHIFT:
Work & the Christian Journey Retreat . . . . *page 260*
by Thomas Bachhuber

Transitions . . . . *page 261*
by Ranier Maria Rilke

A Poem About the Soul . . . . *page 262*
by Mary Oliver

Disappointment . . . . *page 265*
by Tony Hoagland

Lord, I Have Time . . . . *page 267*
by Michel Quoist

Patient Trust . . . . *page 269*
by Pierre Teilhard de Chardin

A Poem on Dreaming . . . . *page 270*
by Teresa of Avila

Who Am I? . . . . *page 271*
by Dietrich Bonhoeffer

For a New Beginning . . . . *page 273*
by John O'Donohue

God of My Life . . . . *page 274*
by Karl Rahner, SJ

Starlings in Winter . . . . *page 275*
by Mary Oliver

Making Successful Career/Work Transitions
Twenty-two Random Ideas . . . . *page 277*
by Thomas Bachhuber

PRAYER AT THE BEGINNING OF LIFESHIFT:
WORK & THE CHRISTIAN JOURNEY RETREATS

BY THOMAS BACHHUBER

God of the universe and of our hearts, You who are Mother
and Father to us, we are grateful for this time.

As in all our journeys, You have arrived here long before us; ea-
gerly and patiently waiting in this holy place, this sacred space, to
welcome and assure us that we are not alone. That You will
be with us as we work, play, rest and pray for new direction.

The Psalmist teaches that You know us better than anyone—
our upsides and down, comings and goings. And so you know
we come from busy lives with to-do lists that are too long and
days often peopled with anxieties. You know we strive for answers and long for clarity. We like quick solutions.

So, Holy One, we ask that you still our souls this moment and in
the time ahead so that we listen more carefully; more attentive-
ly, more lovingly to those around us—and to You.

Help us to be patient in our search for answers and comfortable with the questions, knowing there is truth in each. Help us
to be present in this mystery; and strike the right balance among
rest and work and prayer.

Most importantly, help us to live the lyrics of the Carmelite
Paul Gurr—that we come to you just as we are. For that is
how You love us. Just as we are…You love us this moment, this
day, and all days ahead.

TRANSITIONS

RANIER MARIA RILKE

For do you not see how everything

That happens

Keeps on being a beginning since it

Is itself

In a way so beautiful.

These very days of your transition

Are perhaps the time when every

Thing in you

Is working at God...

And think that the least we can do is

To make

God's becoming not more difficult

Than the earth makes it for the Spring

When it wants to come.

A POEM ABOUT THE SOUL

MARY OLIVER

Nobody knows what the soul is.
It comes and goes like the wind over water.

But just as we can name the functions of the wind, so we
can name some of the functions of the soul without presuming
to penetrate its mystery.

The soul wants to keep us rooted in the ground of our own being,
resisting the tendency of other faculties, like the intellect and ego,
to uproot us from who we are.

The soul wants to keep us connected to the community in
which we find life, for it understands that relationships are necessary if we are to thrive.

The soul wants to tell us the truth about ourselves, our world, and
the relation between the two, whether that truth is easy or hard to
hear.

The soul wants to give us life and wants us to pass that gift along,
to become life-givers in a world that deals too much death.

ACTIVITY

Slowly read Mary Oliver's poem on the four functions of the
soul. Reflect on their meaning for your life. Choose one or more
of the following questions for response.

Keeping us rooted in our being:

Write a line describing how your intellect or ego may get in the way of your soul's development.

_____

_____

_____

_____

_____

Connected to community:

Write a line describing how one of your relationships may get in the way of your soul's development.

_____

_____

_____

_____

_____

Telling us truth:
Write a line describing a challenging truth for you to reflect on, talk about or explore.

_____

_____

_____

_____

_____

_____

Giving/passing along life:
Write a line describing what passing along life means to you.

_____

_____

_____

_____

_____

_____

DISAPPOINTMENT

TONY HOAGLAND

I was feeling pretty religious
standing on the bridge in my winter coat
looking down at the gray water:
the sharp little waves dusted with snow,
fish in their tin armor.

That's what I like about disappointment:
the way it slows you down,
when the querulous insistent chatter of desire
        goes dead calm

and the minor roadside flowers
pronounce their quiet colors,
and the red dirt of the hillside glows.

She played the flute, he played the fiddle
and the moon came up over the barn.
Then he didn't get the job, —
or her father died before she told him
        that one, most important thing—

and everything got still.

TRANSPIRATIONS

It was February or October
It was July
I remember it so clear
You don't have to pursue anything ever again
It's over
You're free
You're unemployed

You just have to stand there
looking out on the water
in your trench coat of solitude
with your scarf of resignation
       lifting in the wind.

LORD, I HAVE TIME

MICHEL QUOIST

I went out, God. People were coming and going,
walking and running.
Everything was rushing; cars, trucks, the street, the whole town.
People were rushing not to waste time.
To catch up with time, to gain time.
Good bye, Sir, excuse me, Mam, I haven't time.
I'll come back, I can't wait, I haven't time.
I must end this letter - I haven't time.
I'd love to help you, but I haven't time.
I can't accept having no time.
I can't think, I can't read, I'm swamped, I haven't time.
I'd like to pray, but I haven't time.

You understand, God, they simply haven't the time.
The child is playing, she hasn't time right now...later on...
The schoolboy has his homework to do, he hasn't time...later on...
The students have their courses, and so much work...later on...
The young woman is at her sports, she hasn't time...later on...
The young married man has his new house; he has to fix it up,
he hasn't time...later on...
The grandparents have their grandchildren, they haven't time...later on...
They are dying, they have no...Too late!...They have no more time!

And so all men and women run after time, God.
They pass through life running - hurried, jostled,
overburdened, frantic, and they never get there. They haven't time.
In spite of all their efforts they're still short of time.
Of a great deal of time.

God, you must have made a mistake in your calculations.
There is a big mistake somewhere. The hours are too short, the days are too short.
Our lives are too short.

You who are beyond time, God, you smile to see us fighting it.
And you know what you are doing.
You make no mistakes in your distribution of time to us.
You give each one time to do what you want us to do.
But we must not lose time
waste time, kill time,
For time is a gift that you give us,
But a perishable gift,
A gift that does not keep.

God, I have time,
I have plenty of time,
All the time that you give me,
The years of my life, the days of my years, the hours of my days.
They are all mine.
Mine to fill, quietly, calmly,
But to fill completely, up to the brim.
To offer them to you, that of their insipid water,
You may make a rich
wine as you made once in Galilee.

I am not asking you this morning, dear God,
for time to do this and then that,
but your grace to do conscientiously, in the time that you give,
what you want me to do.

PATIENT TRUST

PIERRE TEILHARD DE CHARDIN

Above all, trust in the slow work of God.

We are quite naturally impatient in everything
to reach the end without delay.
We should like to skip the intermediate stages.
We are impatient of being on the way to something unknown,
something new.
And yet it is the law of progress
that it is made by passing through
some states of instability—
and that it may take a very long time.

And so I think it is with you.
Your ideas mature gradually—let them grow,
let them shape themselves, without undue haste.

Don't try to force them on,
as though you could be today what time
(that is to say, grace and circumstances
acting on your own good will)
will make of you tomorrow.

Only God could say what this new spirit
gradually forming within you will be.
Give Our Lord the benefit of believing
that his hand is leading you,
and accept the anxiety of feeling yourself
in suspense and incomplete.

A POEM ON DREAMING

TERESA OF AVILA

It is a great help in our quest
to have high aspirations,
because often our actions
begin with our thoughts and dreams.
It is not pride to have great desires.
It is the devil who makes us think
that the lives and actions of the saints
are to be admired but not imitated.

…like the saints, we need to be humble
but bold in our pursuit
trusting God and not ourselves.
For Our Lord loves and seeks courageous souls.
Let us not fail to reach our destiny
because we have been too timid.
Too cautious in our desires, because we sought too little.
It is true that I might stumble for trying
to do too much too soon,
but it is also certain that I will never succeed
if I hope for too little or, out of fear of failing, start not at all.

TRANSPIRATIONS

WHO AM I?

DIETRICH BONHOEFFER

Who am I? They often tell me
I stepped from my cell's confinement
Calmly, cheerfully, firmly,
Like a Squire from his country house.

Who am I? They often tell me
I used to speak to my warders
Freely and friendly and clearly,
As thought it were mine to command.

Who am I? They also tell me
I bore the days of misfortune
Equably, smilingly, proudly,
like one accustomed to win.

Am I then really that which other men tell of?
Or am I only what I myself know of myself?
Restless and longing and sick, like a bird in a cage,
Struggling for breath, as though hands were compressing my throat,
Yearning for colors, for flowers, for the voices of birds,
Thirsting for words of kindness, for neighborliness,
Tossing in expectations of great events,
Powerlessly trembling for friends at an infinite distance,
Weary and empty at praying, at thinking, at making,
Faint, and ready to say farewell to it all.

Who am I? This or the Other?
Am I one person today and tomorrow another?
Am I both at once? A hypocrite before others,
And before myself a contemptible woebegone weakling?

Or is something within me still like a beaten army
Fleeing in disorder from victory already achieved?

Who am I? They mock me, these lonely questions of mine.
Whoever I am, Thou knowest, O God, I am thine!

TRANSPIRATIONS

FOR A NEW BEGINNING

JOHN O'DONOHUE

In out of the way places of the heart
Where your thoughts never think to wander
This beginning has been quietly forming
Waiting until you were ready to emerge.

For a long time it has watched your desire
Feeling the emptiness grow inside you
Noticing how you willed yourself on
Still unable to leave what you had outgrown.

It watched you play with the seduction of safety
And the grey promises that sameness whispered
Heard the waves of turmoil rise and relent
Wondered would you always live like this.

Then the delight, when your courage kindled,
And out you stepped onto new ground,
Your eyes young again with energy and dream
A path of plenitude opening before you.

Though your destination is not clear
You can trust the promise of this opening;
Unfurl yourself into the grace of beginning
That is one with your life's desire.

Awaken your spirit to adventure
Hold nothing back, learn to find ease in risk
Soon you will be home in a new rhythm
For your soul senses the world that awaits you.

GOD OF MY LIFE

KARL RAHNER, SJ

Only in love can I find you, my God.
In love the gates of my soul spring open,
allowing me to breathe a new air of freedom
and forget my own petty self.
In love my whole being streams forth
out of the rigid confines of narrowness
and anxious self-assertion, which makes me a prisoner of my
own poverty and emptiness.

In love all the powers of my soul flow out toward you,
wanting never more to return,
but to lose themselves completely in you,
since by your love you are the inmost center of my heart,
closer to me than I am to myself.

But when I love you,
when I manage to break out of the narrow circle of self
and leave behind the restless agony of unanswered questions,
when my blinded eyes no longer look merely from afar
and from the outside upon your unapproachable brightness,
and much more when you yourself, O Incomprehensible One,
have become through love the inmost center of my life,
then I can bury myself entirely in you, O mysterious God,
and with myself all my questions.

STARLINGS IN WINTER

MARY OLIVER

Chunky and noisy,
but with stars in their black feathers,
they spring from the telephone wire
and instantly

they are acrobats
in the freezing wind.
And now, in the theater of air,
they swing over buildings,

dipping and rising;
they float like one stippled star
that opens,
becomes for a moment fragmented,

then closes again;
and you watch
and you try
but you simply can't imagine

how they do it
with no articulated instruction, no pause,
only the silent confirmation
that they are this notable thing,

this wheel of many parts, that can rise and spin
over and over again,
full of gorgeous life.

Ah, world, what lessons you prepare for us,
even in the leafless winter,
even in the ashy city.
I am thinking now of grief,
and of getting past it

I feel my boots
trying to leave the ground,
I feel my heart
pumping hard. I want

to think again of dangerous and noble things.
I want to be light and frolicsome.
I want to be improbable beautiful and afraid of nothing,
as though I had wings.

MAKING SUCCESSFUL CAREER/WORK TRANSITIONS TWENTY-TWO RANDOM IDEAS*

THOMAS BACHHUBER

Making successful career and job transitions involves our complete intellectual, physical, and spiritual selves. The market is replete with books, seminars, web resources, and people claiming to provide "the answer"– or at least a piece of it.

We know there isn't one–just the hard, heart work of continually refining the transition process, procedures and strategies which will lead to a new, satisfying job. Each day, one step at a time.

The following 22 ideas may provide some additional structure and insight to your process. They are placed in 4 major groups:

❖ Maintain Realistic, Positive Outlooks

❖ Determine Your Path

❖ Train Yourself With Job Seeking Essentials

❖ Engage Your Soul Perspective

Perhaps there are some ideas that apply to your transition, helping you enhance or distill what you're doing.

MAINTAIN REALISTIC, POSITIVE OUTLOOKS

1. *Know that the transition process is not predictable or rational.*

   Howard Figler speaks of the Zen of the workplace in his book, *The Complete Job Search Handbook:*

   ❖ Job seeking is not a predictable process,

   ❖ There are unknown and hidden variables,

   ❖ Many things are out of your control.

   Scientific, rational methods only go so far and are only part of the solution. Think out of the box; take calculated chances. Sometimes do something because it just feels "right."

2. *Accept what is.*

   It takes us away from the negativity that is often in our mind and moves us toward the truth, which is in our soul. When unemployed or between jobs, this variation on an Eckhart Tolle principle is essential for us to embrace the loss of what was and take productive steps toward what will be. There's little gained by wishing something didn't happen or should be otherwise.

3. *Keep the "mental phantoms" at bay.*

   Tolle defines "mental phantoms" as "what if" statements that are not real and interfere with positive thinking and action. The mind projects itself into imaginary situations and creates fear. Phantoms can also include unproductive self-talk like "I shouldn't have taken that opportunity," "I deserve better," "It might have been different if," "He or she could have done," "I ought to have said that better." You get the idea.

4. *Know in your heart that you have gifts which the world needs.*

"Giftedness is the only means I know of for the ordinary person to make sense out of life. Each one is given a purpose and the drive and competitiveness to achieve that purpose. Meaning is thereby built into the adventure of living for everyone."(Arthur Miller). Focusing on how you can contribute to organizations, causes, other lives is a key practice.

5. *In losing a job, recognize it is a death.*

Get upset, angry; grieve; and know it's characterized by stages of denial, anxiety, confusion, uncertainty, action and new beginnings. Believe in your best, strongest self and that you will survive it– and even thrive in the new opportunities which you will discover. Parker Palmer encourages us to be more comfortable with death as one of his five "shadow-casting monsters" as it relates not just to our own mortality but to ideas, projects, relationships. Everything new began because something ended.

6. *Don't go it alone.*

This transition work is hard and complicated. Seek out a trusted coach, counselor, and advisor or mentor to help you. When things get overwhelming and complex, it's usually essential to get help. Your coach or mentor can be invaluable in helping you determine what help should look like.

7. *Don't let the media statistics on the economy and job market discourage your job seeking.*

Much of the data is not applicable to your personal situation or solution–it certainly may have a negative influence on your opportunities but there are many positive factors to consider as well. Don't use the situation as an excuse, but rather as a challenge. Focus on the positive may seem like simple advice but don't underestimate how critical it can be to your attitude—and well-being.

DETERMINE YOUR PATH

8. *Discern your mission in life as central to your decision-making as you look to new opportunities.*

"Decide" has the same root as homicide - to kill off or eliminate. "Discern" means to look beyond physical vision and encourages the deeper identification of your passions–your most valued skills and interests. Studs Terkel line from *Working*, "We work for daily meaning and our daily bread," brings home this need to go expand horizons when in transition.

9. *Have a written vision or mission statement—a long-term plan for how your life will be better and more meaningful through work and life work balance.*

Balance realism and fantasy. Have heart in your goals, but know that plans must be clear and have measurable milestones; a mentor and leader can be a great help in guiding and supporting you. Striking the balance between fulfilling your dreams and identifying employers who will pay you for the value you add and skills you have is difficult but critical.

10. *Self-assessment is always necessary for successful planning, i.e. clarifying and communicating your career interests, skills and values.*

But most often, the fog lifts and the sun rises on career indecision once you are out there in the marketplace – experiencing, exploring, examining and experimenting. INSEAD Professor Herminia Ibarra's wisdom here is spot on:

> "We learn who we have been and who we might become —in practice, not in theory–by testing fantasy and reality, through exploration and examination, not just by looking inside. Knowing oneself is critical, but it is usually the outcome of–and not a first input to–the reinvention process. Intense introspection poses the danger that a potential career planner will get stuck in the realm of daydreams."

11. *There is no perfect job–life has always been about tradeoffs.*

You'll make many as you evaluate job roles, responsibilities, organizational culture, colleagues, management styles, management hierarchy, benefits, etc., etc. But a compromise job can lead to a good one later. So…it's the evaluation process which matters–and being clear on your priorities. Career planning usually involves dealing with abstract possibilities but when specific jobs are identified and eventually offered, then concrete criteria–and tradeoffs– come into play. And choices can be more realistically and intelligently made.

12. *Place job market projections in the proper context.*

They are one variable of countless in determining your strategies and plans. Job market statistics are aggregate data–they cross all industries and make up the 20,000 foot view. Each job hunter must define his or her own personal or ground level job market – the openings, opportunities, and organizations where your skills and background match.

TRAIN YOURSELF WITH JOB SEEKING ESSENTIALS

---

13. Place job loss and/or career change in appropriate context.

It's extremely tough on the ego as much of our identity is tied up with work, but you will both lose and gain good things as you move toward fresh opportunities. There will be tradeoffs and you'll gain many useful life lessons. The transition experience will be invaluable to your life–and is usually more prized in retrospect. William Bridges' phrase "re-invent yourself" is accurate and exciting as you move into new environments.

Jack Falvey says you must be the head of both sales and research in your job-seeking company. As head of research, you uncover through micro-research techniques (web, print, people) the key issues, ideas and questions around which to build your discussions. It's through these information—seeking meetings that you will impress others and increase your credibility. In these situations, people want to help you, resulting in referrals and discussions turn to recruitment. That is the essence of Richard Bolles' best selling trade book, *What Color Is Your Parachute?* It's been telling the truth since 1974!

14. Job hunting should be called job slogging.

You will have ups and downs, dark and light moments; days of consolation—days of desolation. There's little glamorous, efficient or streamlined about the process–and there are lots of detours. Every "no" brings you closer to the "yes." You will be successful in getting something better or a step toward better. It can be helpful to allow yourself to be ok with and even welcoming to "purposeless wandering." Taoists call it wu-wei—allowing space within and around me so conflict and confusion can settle and a deeper wisdom emerge. Guidelines and a generous timetable can enhance this process. This is also compatible with Herminia Ibarra's emphasis on exploring and experimentation.

15. *Master in the job search that which you can.*

You can't do everything perfectly. We're human beings with many flaws. Parker Palmer encourages us to "honor our limitations." That translates to working around them—and getting help where we need it. The basic job seeking tasks need to be done as well as you can—identifying and articulating your strengths, conducting thorough job research, using multiple job-seeking strategies, preparing for interviews, asking great questions, seeking support and assistance from valued mentors and coaches, planning for the unexpected, and having back-up options in place.

16. *The web isn't the answer.*

It's a tool or resource. Yes, you have to continually bang away on the best job boards and employer websites for you. But most importantly, use the web to research key intelligence about employers and how it relates to you. You have to apply for positions within the electronic systems set by employers. They make the rules, but know it's the human touch that will make the difference between success and failure. You will get a good job because you and an employer have a mutually satisfying communication. Jack Falvey says you have to be out in the cold damp rain if you're going to get struck by lightning. That means out there where employers are – virtually and in person.

17. *Prepare, prepare and prepare for the tasks you are able to control and manage:*

❖ Craft and send clear, concise communications to employers,

❖ Write and speak about the specific connections between your strengths and employer needs – employers will not do it for you,

❖ Have a cover letters, emails and a resume that make the "business case" for your candidacy—business case is about evidence and examples,

❖ Make crisp email, text and telephone contacts with industry specific language,

❖ Network for informational interviews as a key strategy for making contacts – it's not just about identifying job opportunities in the hidden job market but rather impressing people with your research about salient issues and ideas which translate to in-depth questions. Job opening and vacancy information comes later,

❖ Interview with planning behind it—know what you need to answer and ask. Balance preparation with spontaneity. This is not easy but your techniques improve with practice in non-interviewing situations. Even the best communicators don't perform well in interviews when they don't prepare enough.

18. *The Job Market is Unfair.*

Although we know this in our head, it rarely makes it to our heart. We keep hoping there's a recipe and if we mix all the ingredients in the right proportion we will wind up with that award-winning cake. Understanding this truth can cut down on the heartache when the offer doesn't come – and avoid some of the self-blame that is only counterproductive:

❖ The "best" candidate only sometimes gets the job,

❖ There are unpredictable elements and things you just can't control like business outcomes, personal agendas, political schemes, etc.,

❖ Sometimes you won't know the reasons for being turned down,

❖ You can do everything right and not get the job.

19. *It's helpful to be both an artist and a scientist to be successful in career transition and job seeking.*

Artists are creative, spontaneous, imaginative, sensitive, entertaining, and innovative. Scientists are organized, experimental, procedural, systematic, and follow proven theory. All these qualities come into play with varying amounts, nuances and priorities as the situation dictates and all can have a positive impact on job search success.

ENGAGE YOUR SOUL PERSPECTIVE

---

20. *Embrace the hard "heart work" of achieving meaning, breadth and depth in your life because job and career is integral to happiness.*

In the latest of Thomas Merton's journal books, *The Intimate Merton*, Patrick Hart, his secretary and editor, says that at one point Merton realized that he would not find God in the Central American monastery he was hoping to find but rather in the "hard heart work" of being in the room where he woke up every day and moving through his day—falling down, getting up, falling down and getting up again. Finding life/career meaning is no different.

21. *You are encouraged to bring your God, faith or spirit into the transition journey.*

"If you're in a career transition and you have an old faith hanging in the closet of your heart, now would be a good time to take it out and dust it off" (Richard Bolles) Most of us think of faith in something beyond ourselves or the earth we stand on—but faith in self, community, organizations, family and friends and how God is connected to all can be valuable. Consider your spiritual self and be open to support, guidance and strength from new places. (Teilhard de Chardin Jesuit theologian, philosopher and paleontologist) said we are "first spiritual beings who have a human existence, not simply human beings with spiritual opportunities."

22. *French philosopher, Descartes said "I think, therefore I am." Eckhart Tolle counters with, "That's exactly the problem."*

We think many things that aren't helpful or truthful. Tolle says that if we step back and become the "watchful observer" of our thoughts we are more likely to find "truths" in that "space" between us as the observer and the thought itself. Of course, you must use your imagination to do this.

> As you recall thoughts like "I can't," "It won't work," "That's not me," or "I'm not good enough"—they may not be coming from our best selves or our soul. Parker Palmer calls the soul "that lifegiving core of living self, with its hunger for truth and justice, love and forgiveness."

*Handout used in the Center for Life Transitions workshop, Job Search Courage

BIBLIOGRAPHY

Aschenbrenner, George A. *Stretched for Greater Glory-What to Expect from the Spiritual Exercises.* Chicago: Loyola Press, 2004

Avila, Teresa. *The Interior Castle.* Mahwah, NJ: Paulist Press, 2007

Baer, Ulrich, *The Wisdom of Rilke: The Poet's Guide to Life,* New York, NY, The Modern Library, 2005

Began, Jaqueline Syrup, *Schwan, Marie, Praying with Ignatius of Loyola,* Winona MN, St. Mary's Press, 1991

Bolles, Richard, *What Color is Your Parachute?,* Berkeley, CA, Ten Speed Press, 1970- 2009

Bridges, William, *Transitions: Making Sense of Life Changes,* Reading, MA Addison Wesley Publishing, 1980, Da Capo Press, 2004

D'Arcy, Paula, Daybreaks, *Daily Reflections for Lent and Easter,* Liguori, MO, Liguori Publications, 2007

Deignan, Kathleen, *Thomas Merton: A Book of Hours,* Notre Dame, IN, Sorin Books, 2007

Delp, Alfred, S J, *Prison Writings, Introduction by Thomas Merton,* Maryknoll, NY, Orbis Books, 2004

Emerson, Matthew. *"Merton and the True Self"* in America Magazine (online) 2013

Farnham, Suzanne G., Gill, Joseph, McLean, R.Taylor, Ward, Susan M., *Listening Hearts: Discerning Call in Community*, Harrisburg, PA, Morehouse Publishing, 1977, 1994

Farnham, Suzanne G., Joseph P. Gill, R. Taylor McLean, and Susan M. Ward. *Listening Hearts: Discerning Call in Community.* Harrisburg, PA: Morehouse Publishing, 1998

Farra, Harry, *The Little Monk*, New York, NY and Mahwah, NJ, Paulist Press, 1994

Farra, Harry. *The Little Monk.* Mahwah, NJ: Paulist Press, 1994

Figler, Howard E. *The Complete Job Search Handbook*, Henry Holt and Company LLC, New York, 1979

Fleming, David L., SJ. *Draw Me into Your Friendship: A Literal Translation and Contemporary Reading of The Spiritual Exercises.* Institute of Jesuit Sources, 1996

Foster, Robert. *Prayer.* New York: HarperCollins, 1998.

Hart, Patrick, Montaldo, Jonathan, *The Intimate Merton: His Life from His Journals*, San Francisco, Harper Collins, 1999

Hart, Patrick and Jonathan Montaldo, editors. *The Intimate Merton: His Life from His Journals.* San Francisco: Harper San Francisco, 1998

Ibarra, Herminia, *Working Identity: Unconventional Strategies for Reinventing Your Career*, Boston, MA, Harvard Business School Press, 2003

Ibarra, Herminia. *Working Identity: Unconventional Strategies for Reinventing Your Career.* Boston: Harvard Business School Press, 2003

Lowney, Chris, *Heroic Living,* Chicago, IL, Loyola Press, 2009

Lustbader, Wendy. *Life Gets Better: The Unexpected Pleasure of Growing Older.* New York: TarcherPerigree, 2011

Manney, Jim. *God Finds Us.* Chicago: Loyola Press, 2013

Martin, James, S J, *Jesus, A Pilgrimage,* New York, NY, Harper Collins Publishers, 2014

Merton, Thomas. *The Seven Story Mountain.* New York: Harcourt, 1948

Merton, Thomas. *Thoughts in Solitude.* New York: HarperCollins, 1956

Merton, Thomas, *Thoughts in Solitude,* New York NY, The Noonday Press, 1956, 1958

Merton, Thomas, *New Seeds of Contemplation,* New Directions Publishing Corporation, New York, NY,1961

Merton, Thomas. *Conjectures of a Guilty Bystander.* New York: Penguin Random House, 1968

Merton, Thomas. *Choosing to Love the World: On Contemplation.* Louisville, CO: Sounds True, Inc. 2008

Norris, Kathleen. *The Cloister Walk.* New York: Riverhead, 1996

Nouwen, Henri, *The Inner Voice of Love: A Journey Through Anguish to Freedom,* New York, NY, Doubleday, 1996

Nouwen, Henri. *The Inner Voice of Love: A Journey Through Anguish to Freedom.* New York: Doubleday, 1996

O'Brien, Kevin, S J, *The Ignatian Adventure,* Chicago, IL Loyola Press, 2011

Palmer, Parker. *Let Your Life Speak: Listening to the Voice of Vocation.* San Francisco: Jossey-Bass, 1999

Palmer, Parker J., *Healing the Heart of Democracy, ie Courage to Create a Politics Worthy of the Human Spirit,* San Francisco, Jossey Bass, 2011

Palmer, Parker J., *Let Your Life Speak: Listening for the Voice of Vocation,* San Francisco, Jossey-Bass, 2000

Palmer, Parker J., *A Hidden Wholeness The Journey Toward An Undivided Life,* San Francisco, Jossey-Bass, 2004

Palmer, Parker. *On the Brink of Everything: Grace, Gravity & Getting Old.* Oakland: Berrett-Koehler Publishers, 2018

Quoist, Michel, *Prayers,* Kansas City, MO, Sheed and Ward, 1963

Rilke, Ranier Maria. *Letters to a Young Poet.* New York: W.W. Norton & Company, 1954

Rupp, Joyce, OSM, *Little Pieces of Light,* New York, NY/ Mahwah, NJ, Paulist Press, 1994

Smith, Carol Ann, SHCJ, Merz, Eugene F., SJ, *Moment by Moment: A Retreat in Everyday Life* (Ignatian exercises) Notre Dame, IN, Ave Maria Press, 2000

Smith, Carol Ann, SHU and Eugene F. Merz, SJ. *Moment by Moment: A Retreat in Everyday Life.* Notre Dame, Indiana: Ave

Maria Press, 2000

Sneck, William J. SJ, Ph.D. *Struggling with Shame, Anger, Guilt.* St. Paul, MN: Audible Audiobook, 2004

Sparough, J. Michael, SJ, Tim Hipskind, SJ, and Jim Manney. *What's Your Decision? How to Make Choices with Confidence and Clarity.* Chicago: Loyola Press, 2010.

Sweeney, Joe, *Networking is a Contact Sport*, Dallas, TX, 2010

Teresa of Avila, *The Interior Castle*, translation by Kiran Kavanaugh, OCD and Otilio Rodriguez, OCD, Mahwah, NJ, Paulist Press, 1979

Tolle, Eckhart, *A New Earth, Awakening to Your Life's Purpose*, London, Eng, Penguin, 2006

Young, William S J, *St. Ignatius' Own Story* (as told to Luis Gonzales de Camara), Chicago, IL, Loyola University Press, 1956

TRANSPIRATIONS

INDEX

Numbers

1 Corinthians 13:4-7
love 36

2 Corinthians 12:10
strong . . . . XVIII, 51

A

Action, taking
action, taking 238

Adults, older
adults, older 243
guidelines 244

Aschenbrenner, George
George Aschenbrenner 224
Stretched for Greater Glory 224

B

Beatles
"All You Need Is Love" 36, 184

Bolles, Richard
Dick Bolles . . . . XXI, 203, 204
Richard Bolles 144, 282, 286, 303
What Color Is Your Parachute? 282

Bonhoeffer, Dietrich
Dietrich Bonhoeffer 162, 271
Who Am I? 271

Bridges, William
change and transitions 3
endings, grief 20, 24
middles, seeds of hope 78
model for transitions 5–6
reinvented self 198
William Bridges . . XII, XIV, 3, 5, 16, 20, 24, 78, 198, 282, 303

Brown, Judy
The Trough 92

Buechner, Frederick
deepest hunger 162

C

Call, discerning
call, discerning 227

Career/Work Transitions, Successful
Determine Your Path 280
Engage Your Soul Perspective 285
Maintain Realistic, Positive Outlooks 278
Train Yourself With Job Seeking Essentials 282

Carthusians
Ever Ancient, Ever New 201

Chambers, Oswald
My Utmost for His Highest 132
next thing, your 251
Oswald Chambers 4, 8, 132, 251

Children
children . . . 2, 143, 144, 172, 181, 202, 207, 235, 240, 250, 299
Matthew 11:25-27 143
Matthew 18:2-4 143

Cleopas
Luke 24:13-35 107

Colloquy
colloquy 242

Crafton, Barbara
Barbara Crafton 52
Geranium Farm 165

D

D'Arcy, Paula
fear 32
love 167
Paula D'Arcy 16, 32, 167
true self, Daybreaks 16

Decision-making/Discernment
decision-making/discernment 231
research in 234

Delp, Alfred SJ
Jesuit Alfred Delp 255

E

Elijah
  1 Kings 19 92
Examen
  examen. 241

F

Falvey, Jack
  best networking article. 88
  foxhole religion 144, 244
  head of both sales and research 282
  in the rain. 88
  Jack Falvey 88, 144, 244, 282, 283
Fleming, David L., SJ
  David L. Fleming 246
  Draw Me into Your Friendship: A Literal Translation and
  Contemporary Reading of The Spiritual Exercises 246
Ford, Michael
  Michael Ford 137
Foster, Richard
  Richard Foster. 223, 236

G

Galsworthy, John
  John Galsworthy. 78
Gnostic Faith
  Nag Hamaradi Scriptures 43

H

Harrington, Daniel J.
  Daniel J. Harrington. 191
  parable definition 191
Hays, Daniel
  Daniel Hays 184
  Moms. 184
  My Old Man and the Sea 184
Heaven
  heaven, afterlife 35, 201
Heppner, Mary
  Career Transition Inventory 40
  Mary Heppner 40

Hirshfield, Jane
  Everything is connected 254
  Jane Hirshfield 254
Hoagland, Tony
  Disappointment. 265
  Tony Hoagland 265

I

Ibarra, Herminia
  engaging experience 238
  exploring and experimenting 281
  Herminia Ibarra 281
  thinking our way 244
  Working Identity: Unconventional Strategies for Reinventing Your Career. 235
Ignatian Spirituality
  Related to Transition. 241
Ignatius Loyola
  biography. 215
  call 128
  consolation and desolation. 197, 231
  emotions and feelings, consolation, desolation 4
  Ignatian Spiritual Work: Active Reflections. 246
  image of God 221
  imagination, using. 223
  in Transition model 6
  longing 162, 231
  magis, the greater. 5
  motions of the soul 231
  passions, yours 280
  in What's Your Decision? How to Make Choices with
  Confidence and Clarity. 232
  spiritual exercises. 215, 223, 246
  false spirits. 250
  God's loving invitation 251
  good spirits. 249
  motions of the soul. 231, 246
  passions. 280
  what we really want, God wants 163
Interviewing
  interviewing. 88, 116, 151, 284
Isbister, Mary
  General Metal Works. 136
  Mary Isbister. 136

L

LinkedIn

LinkedIn 32, 48, 78, 84, 92, 132, 151, 203, 237

Lombardi, Vince

Vince Lombardi 154

Lord's Prayer

Lord's Prayer, The 27

Lowney, Christopher

Christopher Lowney 162

Heroic Leadership and Pope Francis: Why He Leads the
Way He Does 162

Lustbader, Wendy

Life Gets Better 243

Wendy Lustbader 243

M

Magis

magis (Ad majoram Dei gloriam) 242

Manney, James

God Finds Us 163, 225

Jim Manney 163, 225, 238, 291

Martin, James, SJ

James Martin 191

Jesus: A Pilgrimage 191

McBrien, Richard

Richard McBrien 159

spirituality 159

Merton, Thomas

and Ignatius Loyola 218

Arthur Miller 120

Buddhist colleagues, Tibet 112

home with God 123

Hopkins, Gerald Manley 217

Intimate Merton, The 217, 218, 288

long interior struggle, no apparent constraint 218

obscure call 97

peace from dissatisfaction 136

pointe vierge 254

red, not blood red 165

saved by relationships 194

Seven Story Mountain 217

silence and solitude 221

slow heart work 154

soul, true self 56

stronger than I think 101

Thomas Merton 4, 56, 97, 101, 112, 123, 136, 154,
193, 217, 228, 285, 287, 303

true self 228

truth of our work 193

vocation 154

Why You Can't Be Anything You Want To Be 120

Merz, Eugene, SJ and Carol Ann Smith

Moment by Moment: A Retreat in Everyday Life 246

Model for Transition

Model for Transition 219, 220

Monk, little

Little Monk, The 242

Moses, Yahweh

Moses, Yahweh 159

N

Networking

art and science 88
best article, Jack Falvey 88
chemistry 116
giving not getting 28
networking .... XIX, 9, 28, 30, 32, 84, 88, 102, 116, 128, 136, 203, 233, 234, 237, 240, 244
Networking is a Contact Sport, Joe Sweeney 28
people want to help 282
polished and genuine 64
questions, importance of 28
saying the right thing, conversation 140
true networking 88, 234

New Jersey

New Jersey, Garden State 47

Norris, Kathleen

Cloister Walk, The 224
Kathleen Norris 224

Nouwen, Henri

disempowered 124
Henri Nouwen 4, 36, 124, 184, 232
Inner Voice of Love, The 36, 232
living with or without God 232
love, The Inner Voice of Love 36

O

O'Donnell, J.T.

job dissatisfaction 68
J.T. O'Donnell 68

O'Donohue, John

For Absence 72
For a New Beginning 273
John O'Donohue 72, 259, 273

Oliver, Mary

A Poem About the Soul 262
Mary Oliver 4, 10, 162, 164, 259, 262, 275, 303
soul 162, 262
Starlings in Winter 275

P

Pagano, Chuck

Chuck Pagano 73, 111
head coach of the Indianapolis Colts 73

Palmer, Parker
   death, ending 279
   depression 102
   honor our limitations 150, 283
   my true life 162
   On the Brink of Everything: Grace, Gravity & Getting Old 245
   Parker Palmer . . . . VII, IX, 4, 56, 60, 102, 150, 162, 241, 245, 279, 283, 286, 303
   soul 286
Paul, apostle love,
   1 Corinthians 13:4-7 36
   spirit prays for us, Romans 8: 26-27 158
   stronger, 2 Corinthians 12:10 51
Proverbs
   Proverbs 3:13-15, wisdom 162
Psalms
   Psalm 23, restores my soul 31
   Psalm 42, deep calls to deep 31

Q
Questions, Big
   big questions 222
Quoist, Michel
   Lord, I Have Time 267
   Michel Quoist 267

R
Rahner, Karl, SJ
   God of My Life 274
   Karl Rahner 274
Rilke, Ranier, Maria
   Be patient 229
   Rainer Maria Rilke 229
   Transitions 261
Rupp, Joyce
   Joyce Rupp . . . . VII, XI, 4, 77, 80, 303
   Little Pieces of Light Darkness & Personal Growth 80

S
Sacred Space
   Sacred Space 158
Schein, Edgar
   organizational culture, Merck 173

Smith, Carol Ann & Eugene Merz
Moment by Moment: A Retreat in Everyday Life. 246
Sneck, William, SJ
Struggling with Shame, Anger, Guilt. 226
William Sneck, SJ. 226
Stephen
in Acts, resisting the Spirit. 56
Sweeney, Joe
Joe Sweeney. 28, 88
Networking is a Contact Sport 88

T

Teilhard de Chardin
Patient Trust 269
Teilhard de Chardin 158, 269, 286
Teresa of Avila
Interior Castle, The 233
Poem on Dreaming, A 270
Teresa of Avila 259, 270, 291
Terkel, Studs
Working 280
Thomas, Dylan
Dylan Thomas 243
Tolle, Eckhart
acceptance, true Being. 16, 278
Eckhart Tolle 16, 24, 278, 286
self-defeating messages, phantoms 24, 278
watchful observer. 286
True Networking
True Networking 88

V

Vocation
calling, searching 243
vocation. 225

W

White, Ronald C.
American Ulysses: A Life of Ulysses S. Grant 172
Ronald C. White. 172
Whyte, David
David Whyte. 98, 100
Faith. 98

Willimon, William

William Willimon 48

Wiman, Christian

Christian Wiman 83

Every Riven Thing 83

Work of Transition

work of transition 92, 102, 103, 107, 112, 159, 184, 193, 221, 244

NOTES

ABOUT THE AUTHOR

Dr. Thomas Bachhuber is President of the Board and Executive Director of The Center for Life Transitions, Inc. *His LifeSHIFT: Work and the Christian Journey* weekend retreat is offered throughout the country, combining career/work/retirement planning with spiritual exploration. He serves on the leadership team for the Ignatian Volunteer Corps Milwaukee and volunteers as a Eucharistic Minister at St. Luke's Hospital, Milwaukee.

Tom was Director of the Career Development Center at the University of Wisconsin-Milwaukee and also the University of Maryland-College Park. He held an Adjunct Faculty position in UWM's Educational Psychology Department. As a consultant, he provided training, research and recruitment strategies for Fortune 500 companies like Merck, Pfizer, Kraft Foods, Deloitte and Touche, Pepsi Cola Bottling and Goldman Sachs.

Besides, TRANSPIRATIONS, Dr. Bachhuber's published books include *Directions: a Guide to Career Planning* (Houghton-Mifflin), *A Parent's Guide to Helping Their Children with Educational and Career Decisions* (Abbey Press) and three editions of the *The Best Graduate Business Schools* (Macmillan/Simon Schuster).

Tom was an elder at North Branch Reformed Church in North Branch, New Jersey, where he counseled seminarians and led workshops at New Brunswick Theological Seminary. Tom's Doctorate and Masters in Counseling are from the University of Virginia. He and Leslie have been married for almost 50 years. They have three adult children, Libby, Emily and Jay and one grandchild, Oona Mae.

CENTER FOR
LIFE TRANSITIONS

The Center for Life Transitions, Inc. was founded in North Branch, New Jersey by Tom and his friend Scott Pontier in 2002, as a non-profit 501©3 to help people in transition find new, meaningful direction in their life/work while exploring their faith and spirituality. The Center moved to Milwaukee, Wisconsin in 2012 under Tom's leadership.

LifeSHIFT: Work & the Christine Journey is the Center's signature program and is a weekend retreat offered at several sites including Wisconsin, Minnesota, Kansas, Pennsylvania and California. The Center is also developing a web-based program, *The Ignatian Way: A Map for Work & Spiritual Exploration*, which applies Ignatius of Loyola's ministry throughout Europe as a framework for people in transition. In the various cities, people will engage in work planning and spiritual activities while learning about Ignatius' life and spirituality.

Contact: Thomas Bachhuber, Ed.D.

tom@centerforlifetransitions

The Ignatian Volunteer Corps® (IVC) provides men and women, most age 50 or better, opportunities to serve others and to transform lives. IVC matches the talents of experienced Volunteers with the greatest social needs of our time. IVC works in partnership with hundreds of community partner organizations. These nonprofit organizations provide Ignatian Volunteers with substantive work to serve individuals who have slipped through this country's safety net. And hundreds of community organizations are on waiting lists to get an Ignatian Volunteer.

Volunteers are strengthened in their Christian faith by IVC's unique spiritual reflection program, which is rooted in the Jesuit tradition of Ignatian Spirituality.

By contributing their leadership skills and life experience into service, IVC volunteers improve their communities and create a more just society.

For information: www.ivcusa.org

TRANSPIRATIONS
GUIDANCE FOR THE HEAD & HEART
THROUGH CAREER & BEYOND

TRANSPIRATIONS is an invaluable educational and spiritual companion for anyone in job, career or retirement transition. Dr. Bachhuber brings leading career/work insights from experts like William Bridges, Richard Bolles, and Herminia Ibarra together with his experience, expertise and personal memories. He weaves the wisdom of important spiritual writers like Thomas Merton, Henri Nouwen, Mary Oliver, Ignatius of Loyola, Parker Palmer, Teresa of Avilia and Sister Joyce Rupp into his spiritual and personal experiences. The book will educate, edify and encourage the reader.

You may find the book helpful, if you are:

❖ Approaching or experiencing retirement and searching for new meaning in your next work, volunteer, and/or ministry opportunity,

❖ Experiencing dissatisfaction with your career/work/ministry and looking for fresh perspectives and purpose,

❖ Feeling unsatisfied at the beginning or middle of a career and looking for a new direction,

❖ Desiring to look inward and use spiritual ideas/resources to help with discernment,

❖ Needing encouragement, inspiration and a closer relationship between your transition work and your faith/spiritual life,

❖ Going through a challenging time professionally, emotionally and/or spiritually.

CPSIA information can be obtained
at www.ICGtesting.com
Printed in the USA
BVHW040859170622
639751BV00008B/15